fire ^{to} fire

ALSO BY MARK DOTY

POETRY

School of the Arts
Source
Sweet Machine
Atlantis
My Alexandria
Bethlehem in Broad Daylight
Turtle, Swan

MEMOIR AND NONFICTION

Dog Years
Still Life with Oysters and Lemon
Firebird
Heaven's Coast

fire *to* fire

new and selected poems

MARK DOTY

HARPER ● PERENNIAL

NEW YORK ● LONDON ● TORONTO ● SYDNEY ● NEW DELHI ● AUCKLAND

HARPER ● PERENNIAL

FIRST HARPER PERENNIAL EDITION PUBLISHED 2009.

Designed by Mary Austin Speaker

Library of Congress Cataloging-in-Publication Data is available upon request.

ISBN 978-0-06-075251-4

09 10 11 12 13 WBC/RRD 10 9 8 7 6 5 4 3 2 1

for Paul

Contents

New Poems:
THEORIES AND
APPARITIONS

PIPISTRELLE

His music, Charles writes,
makes us avoidable.
I write: emissary of evening.

We're writing poems about last night's bat.
Charles has stripped the scene to lyric,
while I'm filling in the tale: how,

when we emerged from the inn,
an unassuming place in the countryside
near Hoarwithy, not far from the Wye,

two twilight mares in a thorn-hedged field
across the road—clotted cream
and raw gray wool, vaguely above it all—

came a little closer. Though
when we approached they ignored us
and went on softly tearing up audible mouthfuls,

so we turned in the other direction,
toward Lough Pool, a mudhole scattered with sticks
beneath an ancient conifer's vast trunk.

Then Charles saw the quick ambassador
fret the spaces between boughs
with an inky signature too fast to trace.

We turned our faces upward,
trying to read the deepening blue
between black limbs. And he said again,

There he is! Though it seemed only
one of us could see the fluttering pipistrelle
at a time—you'd turn your head to where

he'd been, no luck, he'd already joined
a larger dark. There he is! Paul said it,
then Pippa. Then I caught the fleeting contraption

speeding into a bank of leaves,
and heard the high, two-syllabled piping.
But when I said what I'd heard,

no one else had noticed it, and Charles said,
Only some people can hear their frequencies.
Fifty years old and I didn't know

I could hear the tender cry of a bat
—*cry* won't do: a diminutive chime
somewhere between merriment and weeping,

who could ever say? I with no music
to my name save what I can coax
into a line, no sense of pitch,

heard the night's own one-sided conversation.
What to make of the gift? An oddity,
like being double-jointed, or token

of some kinship to the little Victorian handbag
dashing between the dim bulks of trees?
Of course the next day we begin our poems.

Charles considers the pipistrelle's music navigational,
a modest, rational understanding of what
I have decided is my personal visitation.

Is it because I am an American I think the bat came
especially to address me, who have the particular gift
of hearing him? If he sang to us, but only I

heard him, does that mean he sang to me?
Or does that mean I am a son of Whitman,
while Charles is an heir of Wordsworth,

albeit thankfully a more concise one?
Is this material necessary or helpful to my poem,
even though Charles admires my welter

of detail, my branching questions?
Couldn't I compose a lean,
meditative evocation of what threaded

over our wondering heads,
or do I need to do what I am doing now,
and worry my little aerial friend

with a freight not precisely his?
Does the poem reside in experience
or in self-consciousness

about experience? Shh,
says the evening near the Wye.
Enough, say the hungry horses.

Listen to my poem, says Charles.
A word in your ear, says the night.

THE WORD

White cotton cap, immaculate shoes
and stockings, black coat over starched dress,
she performs her work, holds the book

open in front of her, looks down
through thick-rimmed glasses, glances up
swiftly so as not to lift her eyes long from the task,
covertly taking stock of who takes stock of her,

spine of the holy text in her left hand,
dark right forefinger tapping a random
or necessary passage, how has she chosen it?

I would say she beats out a jeremiad,
cannot or will not speak and so this iteration
is her form of witness—save that in her insistence
she strikes with the hard tap of her fingernail,

over and over, wearing the ink away until
the thin paper tears, lower half of the pages tatted,
as if mice had been shredding the blessings

and prohibitions for a nest,
no choice but to point to or punish the book or both,
tearing away at the damned loved word
that is everything to her and does not deliver her

and therefore she must go on wounding the book
in public: her art, displayed for us, unvarying,
in the station at 34th Street and Sixth Avenue,

on a bitter night just after the turn of the year.

IN THE AIRPORT MARSHES

A kind of heaven,
this clamor, a *lulliloo*:
"to shout joyously,
to welcome with cries,

from a cry of joy among
some African peoples":
Webster's New International,
1934, a foot-thick volume

deftly marbled
as this patch of marsh.
Today I require the term
and there it is—these definitions

wait to be lived,
actual as these frogs,
who chorus as if
there's no tomorrow,

or else they've all
the time in the world.
We ruin the rain,
they go right on,

this year. Hard to imagine
the eagerness of a body
which pours itself
into *this*—forms

you have to take on faith,
since all they seem
to be is chiming Morse
belling out long-short

over the patched tarmac
of the runway. I never till now
needed the word *lulliloo*.

How do you reckon your little music?

APPARITION (FAVORITE POEM)

The old words are dying,
everyone forgets them,
pages falling into sleep and dust,

dust and sleep, burning so slowly
you wouldn't even know there's a fire.
Or that's what I think half the time.

Then, at the bookstore, a young man reciting,
slight for fourteen, blond, without irony
but not self-important either;

his loping East Texas vowels threaten
to escape the fence of pentameter,
his voice seems to have just arrived here,

but the old cadence inhabits anyway.
He makes the poem his own
even as he becomes a vessel

for its reluctance to disappear.
All right, maybe they perish,
but the boy has the look of someone

repeating a crucial instruction
that must be delivered, word for word,
as he has learned it:

My name is Ozymandias, King of Kings,
Look on my Works, ye Mighty, and despair.

ANGEL OF PRAGUE

I have joined a student theater group,
an insurrection in the motherly gray capital
battered by invasion and occupation

—exhausted somnolence, dreary romance.
In the piece we're mounting,
a demonstration in the central square,
I play the role of the Angel of Prague,

and must climb the façade of an ancient church
fronting the square, and stand behind the statue
of a female figure, a near-forgotten saint,

where I am to unfurl a pair of large fabric wings,
in my dream, my blue wing upon which is written,
IT MUST BE BEAUTIFUL, and my red wing
which reads IT MUST BE NEW.

I hold on to the waist of the statue
until I unfurl the second wing,
and then I must balance

on the narrow pedestal, or lean
against her stone back to support myself,
which is all right until I look down
the cold dizzying stories to the pavement,

and gradually find myself furling
the cloth around her stone shoulders,
my legs trembling; it's hard to hold out

your arms when you're frightened
of being dashed on the stones below,
and in a while I slink down, back into the crowd,
where I shed my huge armature

and am praised for my performance
despite the fact that I feel defeated,
that I have given in to weakness

when I could, if I were stronger and less fearful,
I could have upheld those wings.

CITIZENS

The light turns and I'm stepping
onto the wide and empty crosswalk on Eighth Avenue,
nothing between the white lines but a blowing riffle

of paper when this truck—
all unnecessary red gleam—roars onto the avenue from 20th,
the driver turns his wheels inches from my knees

even though I jump back
out of the way, and before I've even thought I'm yelling
what are you doing, act like a citizen

though it's clear from the face
already blurred past me he's enjoying this, and I shout *Asshole*
and kick at the place where his tire was with my boot.

If I carried a sharp instrument
I could scrape a long howl on his flaming paint job
(just under the gold and looming logo: DEMOLITION)

and what kind of citizen
does this thought make me, quivering and flummoxed
by contradictory impulses: to give a speech on empathy

or fling my double latte
across his back windshield, though who knows what
he might do then. He's stuck in traffic and pretends

I'm not watching him looking
in my direction, and people passing doubtless think who is
this idiot fulminating to himself,

or probably they don't;
they've got trouble of their own. Here's a story:
two pilgrim monks arrive at a riverbank

where an old lady's weeping,
no way to cross, and though they've renounced
all traffic with women, one man hoists her on his shoulders

and ferries her over the water.
Later his friend is troubled: *How could you touch her*
when you vowed not to? And the first monk says, *I put her down*

on the other side of the river,
why are you still carrying her? Midday's so raw and dirty
I can't imagine anyone here's pleased with something just now,

and I'm carrying the devil
in his carbon chariot all the way to 23rd, down into the subway,
roiling against the impersonal malice of the truck that armors
    him

so he doesn't have to know anyone.
Under the Port Authority I understand I'm raging
because that's easier than weeping, not because I'm so afraid

of scraping my skull
on the pavement but because he's made me erasable,
a slip of a self, subject to. How'd I get emptied

till I can be hostaged
by a dope in a flaming climate-wrecker? I try to think
who made him so powerless he craves dominion over strangers,

but you know what?
I don't care. If he's one of those people miserable for lack
of what is found in poetry, fine.

It's not him I'm sorry for.
It's every person on this train burrowing deeper uptown
as if it were screwing further down into the bedrock.

Heavy hands on the knees,
weary heads nodding toward the floor or settling
against the glass. When did I ever set anything down?

APPARITION

Chilly noon on Seventh,
and I swear in the window
of the Eros Diner, corner
of 21st Street,

John Berryman's eating alone,
back against the wall,
face tilted down toward
his meal, iconic thick glasses

glinting like the sidewalk
in the cold, iconic thick beard
nodding a little as he lifts
his spoon, intent

on lunch, so happy
that a plate's in front
of him he never bothers
to look up at me.

HOUSE OF BEAUTY

In Jersey City, on Tonnelle Avenue,
the House of Beauty is burning.

On a Sunday morning in January,
under the chilly shadow of the Pulaski Skyway,
the House of Beauty is burning.

Who lobbed the firebottle through the glass,
in among the crèmes and thrones,
the helmets and clippers and combs,
who set the House of Beauty burning?

In the dark recess beside the sink
—where heads lay back to be laved
under the perfected heads rowed along the walls—
the hopeful photographs of possibility darken,
now that the House of Beauty is burning.

The Skyway beetles in the ringing cold,
trestle arcing the steel river and warehouses,
truck lots and Indian groceries,
a new plume of smoke joining the others,
billow of dark thought rising
from the broken forehead of the House of Beauty

—an emission almost too small to notice, just now,
alarm still ringing, the flames new-launched
on their project of ruining an effort at pleasure,
glass jutting like cracked ice in the window frame,
no one inside, the fire department on the way.
All things by nature, wrote Virgil, *are ready to get worse;*
no surprise, then, that the House of Beauty is burning.

Though whatever happens, however far
these fires proceed, reducing history to powder,
whatever the House of Beauty made is untouchable now;
nothing can undo so many heads made lovely
or at least acceptable, so much shapelessness
given what are called permanents, though nothing holds
a fixed form. Bring on the flames,
what does it matter if the house is burning?

Propose a new beauty, perennially unhoused:
neither the lost things nor the fire itself,
but the objects in their dresses of disaster,
anything clothed in its own passage:
padded vinyl chair burst into smoky tongues,
Lucite helmet sagged to a new version of its dome.
Our black bridge, a charred rainbow on iron legs,
two ruby eyes glowering from its crown.
If beauty *is* burning, what could you save?
The house of beauty is a house of flames.

THEORY OF THE SOUL

Ligustrum, penicillium,
three ragweeds, fusarium, marshelder, pollen of timothy, sweet
    vernal,
cocklebur and feathers, dog and tuna, dust mite, milk and yolk:

the allergist's assistant
pierces the skin of my back with ten clusters of needles,
each dipped in tinctures, and we wait to see which ones make
    me sick.

She says, You're okay, right?
and leaves the room. I'm a little tired, holding my face
in my hands, warm, leaning forward,

and then a doctor says,
How long ago did you give him that shot? A nurse says, Ten
    minutes.
A shot? Adrenaline, the doctor says, you had an allergic
    reaction

to the allergy test.
I thought if you blacked out you'd see it like a movie,
people gathering above your head, but of course I wasn't there

to know I was gone.
Later, when I tell Claudia, she says, How can you know when
    you're not awake?
Ten minutes, no perception—just a little queasy,

then a jump cut
and I'm the hot center of a buzzing host afraid I'll sue them
because they've injected me with solutions of mouse hair,
    lobster and egg,

and left me to my own devices.
I tell Claudia this is what troubles me: I've been around enough
    dying
to trust that last breath wings out something more than air—

But where was I,
or that, if the self's embalmed by an injection of seafood and
    dust?
Animation, intelligence, the gathered weight of half a century

switched off like a lamp?
And then I tell her—well, Claudia isn't even in the room,
I'm talking to the Claudia I carry around in my head,

as we address our friends
in solitary moments, driving or walking uptown to the market—
I don't know why I tell her about the black kid

in the dingy passageway
to the L yesterday singing early Beatles with a radical purity,
everything distilled to a bright arcing liquid vulnerability

spilling over,
and the amaryllis bulbs in the florist's window flinging their
    bodies
forward in order to arrive at red, the single term of their
    arrival—

self made visible
in the reach for a form, breath in this body then
that, passed on or gone, and maybe that's why

we love to kiss,
because then we come closest to the exhaled quick.
We are what we make? Yeah, Claudia says,

all that. But where
is my work, while I'm prone on the allergist's floor?
The doctor who recommends, once I am breathing regularly,

that I avoid oysters,
and encourages me to call him again.

APPARITION

Handsome chest thick with white hair cropped close,
the pleasant man leans the stacked solid volume

of himself back to rest, reclining on his pillows, and I sit back
on my knees to take stock of him, but the look

sucks the breath out of me: he is gazing in my direction
with a pleased half smile, eyes a little out of focus, as though I'm
     seeing him

or he views me through a kind of gauze, and he isn't the man I
     know
—slightly—but, plain as early winter daylight

across the Hudson, the impossible gentle manly visionary
of the eighteen-fifties, bowl-cut hair, warm lines around the eyes

dilated as by an opiate, what shines in
and out of them in equal proportion—

That's the Walt Whitman who has come to look at me,
curiously, on a mild November afternoon on the west side of
     Midtown.

THEORY OF BEAUTY (TONY)

Somebody who worked in the jailhouse kitchen
cooked up some grease, burnt it black, scraped
the carbon from the griddle. Somebody made a needle
from the shaft of a filched Bic, ballpoint replaced

with a staple beaten flat; then the men received,
one at a time, faces of Christ looking up through
streams of blood from a thorny crown,
or death's heads looming over x's of bones.

But Tony chose, for his left shoulder, a sign language
glyph, a simple shape, though hard to read;
he had to tell me what it meant. He flicked
his lighter and spilled flecks of dope on the towel

across his lap, brushed his bare stomach as though
he might have set himself aflame. He said,
It stands for Love. Then what seemed indifferently
drawn, hardly a sketch, became a blazon

that both lifted and exposed the man who wore it,
as he fumbled with the lighter, too stoned to fire
the pipe he held, using it to point to the character
on his arm, making plain the art of what was written there.

THEORY OF BEAUTY (GREENWICH AVENUE)

Thirty-seven clocks in five tiers.

Mantel, cuckoo,
rusticated, ormolu, glass-domed, moving brass balls and chimes,
porcelain, bronze-figured French:
thirty-seven, ranged in the shop window,
not especially attractive,

none fine, none precious,
even to my taste individually desirable.
But studying them, then turning away

into the end of a mild afternoon
the hand of winter's never quite let go of,

warmly tinted but almost heatless sunlight,
buildings ahead in silhouette, and then
the urge to turn back to the stepped rows

and suddenly the preeminently important thing
is their fulfillment of the category *clock*,

the divergence of means
of occupying that name, honoring the terms
and intent of it but nonetheless

presenting a various set of faces
to the avenue, in the warm light
of the shop. Then I or you, whoever's

doing the looking, understands
that this is the city's particular signature,

the range of possibilities within any single set,
and what is pleasing is not the individual clock

(goofy or kitsch, in their frostings and columns,
scrollworks and gildings) but the degree

to which it belongs and at the same time
pushes toward the edges of difference—

so the window's
thirty-seven branching aspects

of a single notion,
almost absurd in their essentially useless variety.
And when you turn away again,

there on the sidewalk
is a perfect instance of the category *sink*,

in this case *kitchen*,
singular instance of all its category
in the five boroughs,

a double stainless model
battered around the drain, humbled at its edges,

rim a little crumpled, but the interior
shining from a lifetime of scouring,

and beauty resides not within
individual objects but in the nearly
unimaginable richness of their relation.

THEORY OF MULTIPLICITY

I don't like the laundromat on 16th Street in the winter,
the single aisle between washers and dryers too narrow
to allow one to sit down, and the women who work there
doing the laundry of others seem to resent one's in-the-wayness,
and why aren't you paying them to do your wash anyway?

But in summer it's fine: you can read on the street, in white
    plastic chairs
set out for this purpose, watch people go by, and, as I liked to do
one summer, look into the garden someone made next door
on the edge of the sidewalk, spilling onto the pavement,
surprisingly wild, with prairie grasses, a shrubby coneflower,
strapping and frowsy black-eyed Susan, even a few bees

frowsing through it— how do they live, in Manhattan?
Leaning back on the legs of the white chair, staring into the green,
I thought of myself as one of its many viewers. What I knew
was this singular aspect, this vantage, in this light,
but didn't its actuality consist in being seen multiply?

Those who did not ignore it in their hurry took it in
from the particular height or angle afforded them,
and even those who paid no mind must have registered,
subtly, the tumbled blur of periphery. What was
the garden but the sum of all that, studied or casual?
Perception carried, loved, considered, dis- or regarded.

Late in the season, frost probably not far off, afternoon
slanting down from the London plane trees, already yellowed
and thinning leaves, sunlight humming into the stalks,
the garden I saw one occasion of many. And this
was in some way an accomplishment,

a contribution to the work; it took all of us
to make the garden known. No one could assemble
the entire vantage we made together.
If anyone could . . . I felt in that moment
not dissolved in anything, not selfless, but joined
in a layering of singularities—a multiplicity

not God, exactly, that theoretical viewpoint,
but a satisfying gesture in that direction.
The next summer the garden would be sparse,
not well tended, and offer no consolation,
though even its diminishment might be said
to be one of its nearly endless dimensions.

THEORY OF BEAUTY (GRACKLES ON MONTROSE)

Eight o'clock, warm Houston night,
and in the parking lot the grackles
hold forth royally, in thick trees

on the lip of traffic, and either
they're oblivious to the street-rush
and come-and-go at the Kroger

or else they actually like it, our hurry
a useful counter to their tintinnabulation.
Now one's doing the Really Creaky Hinge,

making it last a long time;
now Drop the Tin Can, glissando,
then Limping Siren, then it's back

to the Hinge done with a caesura
midstream, so it becomes a Recalcitrant Double Entry.
What are they up to, these late, randy singers,

who seem to shiver the whole tree in pleasure
when somebody gets off a really fierce line,
pirate aerial deejays remixing their sonics

above the median strip all up and down
the block from here to the Taco Cabana?
They sample Bad Brakes, they do

Tea Kettle in Hell, Slidewhistle
into Car Alarm, Firecracker with a Bright Report,
and every feathered body—

how many of them *are* there,

obscured by dense green?
seems to cackle over that one,
incendiary rippling, pure delight,

imperious, impure singing:
traffic in tongues, polyglot,
expansive, awry.

THEORY OF BEAUTY (POMPEII)

Tiny girl in line at the café—seven, eight?—holding her book
    open,
pointing to the words and saying them half-aloud
while her mother attends to ordering breakfast;

she's reading *POMPEII . . . Buried Alive!* with evident delight.
Pleasure with a little shiver inside it.

And that evening, I thought I was no longer afraid
of the death's head beneath the face of the man beneath me.

THEORY OF MARRIAGE

I have a slight thrumming aura of backache,
so Marie—we've met for a late lunch before a movie,
at a Greek place in the West Village—says

What you need is the chi gong parlor,
so we take a cab to a vague block between SoHo and
    Chinatown
—Marie has to look to find it—and once she's spotted

the flight of scarlet stairs leading down from the street,
she leaves us at the door, benevolently, as if to say,
Here, my dears, is the gift I've led you to.

We're ushered into a long room
bright as a nail salon,
various citizens, entirely dressed

but for coat and shoes, prone upon many tables,
as we are, in a moment, Paul an aisle away from me.

His masseur's an intense, strapping man;
mine an intense, compact woman
who asks what sort of treatment I require
and soon pushes against various points
along my spine, knots of tension loosening, and soon I'm fading

under the specific presence of touch; no more bright chamber
full of sore New Yorkers, no more street noise, shoppers,

no more various and polyphonic expressions
of desire, no desire really, just press and release

here and here, awareness moving
from one instance to the next.

Is that the cure, for subjectivity
to diminish to a singular point of attention,
everything but this floated away?

All too soon it's over, and the masseuse says,

Your friend not done, you want do more?
Sure, I say. *Feet,* she says? Almost before I've nodded we're off,
the pushing exploring regions that do not seem

to exist until pressed. And then the self's
a glass fishbowl dropped from some great height,
falling slowly, at ease, shattering

without a sound,

and just as the weightless fish go fantailing free,
I'm aware that Paul is crying, *Ow!*

and then I hear his masseur say, *Your friend not done,*
you want more? And he must think he may as well,
since I am still releasing the contained sounds of one

pushed into new life, until my treatment

comes to an end and the woman says,
Friend not done, we do head?
And as a resistance I didn't know

was there is banished,
I am dimly aware that the masseur
has climbed onto Paul's back, Paul is crying *Oh, ow!*

And just as I am vanishing again into the heaven
of rubbed temples, where no city exists except the one

in which the skull produces a repetitive, golden music,
somewhere far away Paul's masseur says, *your friend* . . .

In this way we spend a small but substantive fortune,

a sum which would have been even greater
had I not cried out, as my masseuse left my hands and wrists
and prepared to commence elsewhere,

Stop, enough, no! To Paul's huge relief,
since he thought I must want to continue,
and therefore he must persist while I am persisting,
even though he was in pain, strong-armed by his assailant,

and I thought he wanted to go on and therefore
I must endure the bliss that had become an exhaustion,

and we walked out onto the street relieved,
late for the movies, Paul limping a little,
my backache gone.

THEORY OF MARRIAGE (THE HUG)

Arden would turn his head toward the one
he loved, Paul or me, and look downward,
and butt the top of his skull against us, leaning forward,
hiding his face, disappearing into what he'd chosen.

Beau had another idea. He'd offer his rump
for scratching, and wag his tail while he was stroked,
returning that affection by facing away, looking out
toward whatever might come along to enjoy.

Beau had no interest in an economy of affection;
why hoard what you can give away?
Arden thought you should close your eyes
to anything else; only by vanishing

into the beloved do you make it clear:
what else is there you'd want to see?

THEORY OF NARRATIVE

Oh, you're a writer, I'm a writer, too, Juan says,
I write novels, I've written eight of them, I'll tell you one.

The sun isn't even up, Juan's driving
our taxi in the high desert north of Mexico City,
I've had no coffee, two hours to the airport in León,
chill air astringent with mesquite smoke and diesel fumes,
there is no coffee in all the world.

This guy, he wants to be a musician, see?
His grandfather encourages him, but his father says,
you must be a doctor, so he goes to medical school,
he studies for years, but there's a revolution,
the clinic's shut down, and he comes home
and finds a hidden note that says,
Dig under the peach tree.
So he gets a shovel and starts digging, everybody comes out
and says what are you doing, are you crazy, there's a revolution,
but he keeps digging, and wrapped in the roots
there's a wooden box, roots are clinging to the box, right?
But he opens the lid, and lifts out a violin,
an instrument his grandfather hid for him,
and when he starts to play it the air fills with the scent of peaches.

This is the beginning of the first story,
a political drama involving the healing powers of the violin,
which lead, after many developments, to the death of Stalin,
and then to the second novel,

a moral fable involving a snake
who swallows a conniving prune,
so that the fruit can sprout in the earth and become a tree,

Early in this tale I realize Juan will not stop,
not for a moment, and Paul is pretending to sleep in the backseat,
so that I seem to be alone with Juan,
and have no other role than assent,

expected to respond at each inquiry—see? right?—
to indicate that I have not ceased to pay the fare
of my attention. Only so much can be done
with the tale of the foolish serpent and wise prune,

out the window unchartable desert
slowly lightening . . . You know? asks Juan,

and suddenly I don't. What am I assenting to,
I am shrinking as each detail is placed into its context,
mmm, uh-huh . . . Has Juan written these stories
at all, is making them up as he drives into
the slow dawning, are we even going toward León?

Now he will try another direction,
and without transition begins the tale
of a woman observed by a frightening voyeur
who sees her every move as she undresses,

and who in the end is revealed—all my stories, Juan says,
are ironical—to be a mosquito,
which she swats, but not before the tiny beast
has infected her with West Nile virus.

A turn that seems to lead down an even darker path
since the next novel's a grotesque family tale
concerning two brothers, one bound in a wheelchair,
and how they plot to poison their vile old father.
But instead of eating the cookies they have prepared for him,

the old guy feeds the arsenical pastries to their own children,
and is even now enjoying his sons' wives, as he writes
in a farewell letter composed in disappearing ink,

because he has committed
the perfect crime, which is this:
I can't get out, have to hear
what happens next, the *further*
of the tires melded to the forwardness of plot.

Is Juan an artist possessed by his work, or a maniac
who wields power through endless, implacable narration?
I cannot look at the great lyric desert
under the new sun because I am hostaged by causality
and chronology, afraid of being put out

in the ditch beside the road,
since the storyteller holds all the power,
and I will not be released
until each character is dead
or meted out an ironical fate,

I am a nodding yes
to a prepossessing will, and is there
an airport anywhere ahead of us,
is there a Leon at all? I can tell you nothing
of the remaining novels. I am party to them,
weakly, as we hurtle past the smolder

of small extinguished grass fires,
citizens awaiting a bus in the cold,
men gathering at an open-air café winking awake
under a string of bulbs hung between wooden posts,
the bodies of dogs struck and lying on the roadside.

(I think Juan himself might have killed them,
driving and driving in the night, telling his endless tales.)

I never want to tell another story, or be told one.
Let the fragments hang in beautiful suspension,
let incident and detail float without ever linking,
I want to be quiet between little ribbons of speech,

since the tyranny of connection
erases the lateral, chains us
to the future, endlessly woven lines
of action I could not begin, now, to remember,
since narrative had gotten what it wanted:

I wasn't there to receive the tale.

Of course we arrived
in mid-story, and Juan pulled over
to the curb and continued to talk,
as if to see how long I would remain listening
while the eighth of his tales wound on,

and when we staggered out of the cab,
hoisting luggage up onto the airport curb,

I was too sick to even feel relieved,
and Paul, gone a pale, peculiar shade
like blanched celery—I do not exaggerate,
although I have, for the sake of a good story—
bent over and vomited onto the sidewalk.

As though we had narrative poisoning,
made to swallow our own medicine
until we choked on it, held too long
to an enlarging mirror
aswarm with vengeful fathers and conniving fruit,
gullible snakes and Orphic musicians,

and even, somewhere, the stuff
of the four other novels which simply refused to register
in my memory.
         —Oh, one more: a man returns
to his old home town,
his grandfather's written him a letter to introduce him
to the spirit of the place,

he's reading only a bit at a time,
on a bench in the public square,
of course he's reading,
moved from moment to moment by
the implacable agency of a narrator,

though the message is half-understood,
never delivered, received partially or late—

so he doesn't understand till the last paragraph
he's already dead, which is why his grandfather says
don't be afraid of the butterflies,

and through a pulsing wall of wings he goes—see?—
into the other side.

APPARITION

Oracular pear,

this peacock
perched in a plywood roost
at the garden center,

magnificent behind a wire fence
marked with his name:
Hommer

(pronounced
without the extra m),
and hand-lettered instructions:

DON'T PROVOKE ME.

He's the provocation:
of what use
the wrought extravagance

he's not just now displaying?
Darwin: "The sight of a feather
in a peacock's tail,

whenever I gaze at it,
makes me sick!"
No reason on earth

even eons of increments

would conspire to this,
and is the peahen
that hard to attract,

requiring an arc of nervous gleams,
a hundred shining animals
symmetrically peering

from the dim
primeval woods?
But if Hommer argues

by his mere presence

for creation, his deity's
a little hysteric,
rampant attitude

contained in all that glory.
Did he who made the lamb
make this imperious

metallic topknot shivering
above an emerald field
of anodized aluminum

while Hommer blinks and flicks

his actual eyes from side to side?
And then the epic
trombone-slide-from-Mars cry

no human throat can mime
—is that why it stops the heart?—
just before he condescends to unfurl

the archaic poem of his tail.

THEORY OF THE SUBLIME

You will, said Carlos, be in my project?

Carlos is a painter who no longer makes use of paint;
his finished work will be a room of monitors,
on each screen a different person clapping;

I am simply to sit and clap my hands together
while Carlos videotapes, for as long as I like.

Beginning's a little awkward,
self-conscious, even though the camera's set on a tripod
and Carlos is hiding his considerable beauty behind a large
    chair;

I'm reaching for some sort of rhythm to perform,
turning my attention away from the afternoon
sunlight in the tall windows of the studio

—but then what simply begins to take place,
a minute into the voyage, *is* a rhythm,
a pattern arising from—the body?—

and the pulse becomes firmer, more persistent,
life of a tree unfurling, green burl spreading out
its swath of selfhood, an actuality:

the clapping is a night-crowd of leaves
billowing out to obscure the quick chips of stars.
The soul occupies the night-town,

reclining in the shadowy chairs, the soil
looms darkly beneath, soul spurts up out of there,
chard raising its green ribs up over a black field

—all signaled, clapped out in the hurry
of one hand sharp against another

rising further until it's alternately praise and outrage,

praise for the world
held against the inevitable
fierce accusation any singularity is,
any lifting individual arc,

that spiraling like climbing the steep winding
of the cathedral in Barcelona, the Sagrada Familia,
stone steps built to the mathematics of a narrow seashell,

feet obscured in darkness, a built night,
and then in a while, many whorls up,
the terrifying small balconies

perched at the back of spires of conch
or chestnut burr or whatever spiked and tiled intensity
the architect pronged from his melting fantasia,

his program of severe transformation,

his enforced (well, no one made me go there,
but once you start up there is no backing out)
passageways into the sublime.

Further, after the little resting platforms,
to strange arched bridges flung between
towering honeycombs,

an unfurled vegetal perch
behind a glazed cypress studded with thick white doves,
up into pinnacles of smashed golden tile.

wounds encrusted in glass, extrusions
of fruit and stone gathering like wax
at the lip of a candle,

I'm mounting a vast beeswax taper,
a honeycombed thing thrusting unlikely,

perfectly solid and somehow entirely unstable.
Far out there is the Mediterranean, tip of a crane,
barking, a dog run down in the square,

sharp green parrots like flying jewels
tussling over scraps of rolls,
and then, at the height of my clapping,
when I can push no further into the thinning air,

perched at a ridiculous and frail slip of masonry
holding together or apart two enameled narwhal tusks
aimed at the next, at the forwardness,

at the limit of praise, when flesh

begins to reassert that it is welded
to the giddy soul trying to get out from the top of the head,

body that's climbed all the way to the tip
of the concrete vertebra
and now contemplates stepping off,

a few tourists snapping photographs as if to hold at bay
the tremendous incipient vertigo and ambition of it.

Then begins the winding
down the towers again,
down swifter than up, light-headed,

body in darkness, flush with the crazy excelsis
of the tower, raked, out of breath, a little sick with all that glory,
stumbling a bit, hands stinging on the railing,

coming to rest, like a pigeon from a long high flight,
as if to land too swiftly and cease the motion of wings
would somehow injure the heart,

so one must land carefully, making out of bare soil
a little container by pressing one's own breast
and belly into the earth,

and when I come to a complete stop the silence
seems extraordinarily firm and authoritative,

and Carlos rises up from behind the tall chair
where he's been hiding to nod his head approvingly,
to indicate that something has happened here,

and in a while I ask how long I've been clapping,
shaking out my stinging hands,

and Carlos looks at his watch and says, Thirty-six minutes,
the room crackling with accusation or prayer.

To what thrills and defeats us: defiance and applause.

TO JOAN MITCHELL

At twilight the locusts begin,
waves and waves,
nothing to do with lamentation.

No one's told them the world is ending;
they proceed as always,
everything subsumed into—

you can't call it a cry, exactly, no singularity in it,
but the thousands, the ten thousand
—voices?

    ✦ ✦ ✦

        Not singing.
Audible undulation, the waves
these bodies make. Seamless, encompassing,
filling Branard Street—

    ✦ ✦ ✦

As it should be.
I want them not knowing,
in this way the sound becomes a kind of refuge,

filled with safety and splendor.

    ✦ ✦ ✦

Or it's more like the big sound
puts its hands under your arms and elevates you,
effortless,
gyrating momentum pulls one upward with it,
collective ululation
having become a unified rising motion

◆ ◆ ◆

            like her great canvas
in four panels,
continuous field so charged
as to fill the room in which it hangs
with an inaudible humming,

as if to erase the gallery over which it triumphs.

Almost audible:

weft of continuous color, blocks of mint,
            green-yellow glaze, olive

floating above a violet
            underpainting, contentious

against the citron and yellow-flung,
            seamless texture,

            like the *hare* of the cicadas,
ceaseless music through which outbreaks of blue

assert themselves.
As if she'd made the human equivalent
    of their spiralling, and this was faith.

◆ ◆ ◆

No trust ever held
    in constancy

—only what's relinquished
    over and over

has about it the heft
    of the genuine—

The canvas firmly centered in its living,
        drenched, upright
            posture of its color—

        the authority of her green

more firmly itself than anyone in the room—

    ◆   ◆   ◆

In the flashpoint summer of 2002
it was possible to feel where we were headed,

sun screwing its titanium compress down
on human foreheads in the parking lots,

thin tamarisks on the margin shimmering a little
as if seen through fumes of gasoline,

and I was in the absolute darkness of Fresno,
past the middle of my life. As if I'd been colonized

by the long swathes of car lots, flapping pennants
stunned under the mercury lamps,

will and inwardness thinned
like the chemical haze over the lettuce fields,

smokes risen from torn-up vineyards,
weary vines heaped for burning . . .

Then a guy in a leather bar—wisdom itself
I swear in an ordinary, bearded face—

held my right hand and stared down
into the contradictory fretwork, drawn

to me and not going home with me,
nothing as simple as that,

though we were two spiked intensities
of pulse and aura, he was holding back

an enormous force of perception,
translating the lines in my palm, and he said

to me the one possible thing I'd believe:
Sometimes you just have to make

a little faith. That fountaining canvas,
expanse of presence in the museum room,

organized and intensified vitality,
ineradicable in spite of the new void we've made

looming everywhere over the vineyards
and shopping centers and car lots from here

to Houston to New York City, relentless, locked in,
poised to erase. The picture spoke its green.

MAGIC MOUSE

Scrap of fur or fabric scrambles hand to hairy wrist,
flees into the hole thumb and forefinger make
in the fist, most warm days, Sixth Avenue and 14th Street:

big-headed guy squats hands outstretched and the toy
slips knuckle to back of the other hand, scurries to the nest
as if of its own volition while he blares over and over

same flat vowels, somehow half the time trumping
layered horns and airbrakes and din of no apparent origin,
raising his terms above the avenue as if he peddled

not the thing itself but its unprintable name:
MAHJIK MAOWWZ,
his accomplishment, a phrase the alphabet refuses.

MAH as in *Nah* as in *No way*, JIK the voice's arc
fallen hard back to the sidewalk, MAOWWZZ
a bridge with a long slide in the center. It won't work

unless you're loud, seal your nasal passages,
inflect five syllables in blat and euphony,
then the little three-syllable follow-through,

price-tag vocalise tailing away like an afterthought:
ONE DOLLAH. Even halfway down the block he's altered
the air, made the spine around which some fraction

of city arranges itself, his beautiful thing
in diminishing coda as you're further away:
Magic Mouse, one dahlah. I practice, I can't

get it right. Maybe what's required is resistance:
indifferent citizens impelled in four directions,
scraps of cell-phone recitations into private ethers,

mechanical sobs his syllables cut through and against.
Maybe it's the sheer persistence of the ugly span
of phrase lifting up and over what it's built to represent.

Or else the engine of his song's the nothing
that could contain that tumbling scrappy model
of a living thing in his hands,

so he says it again and again

—while the little toy, all the word
won't hold, always escaping,
goes on with its astonishing work.

THEORY OF INCOMPLETION

I'm painting the apartment, elaborate project,
edging doorways and bookcases,

two coats at least, and on the radio
—the cable opera station—something
I don't know, Handel's *Semele*,

and either it's the latex fumes or the music itself
but I seem never to have heard anything so radiant,

gorgeous rising tiers of it
ceasing briefly then cascading again,
as if baroque music were a series of waterfalls

pouring in the wrong direction, perpetually up
and up, twisting toward the empyrean.

When a tenor—playing the role of a god,
perhaps the god of art?—calls for unbridled joy
the golden form of his outburst

matches the solar confidence of its content,
and I involuntarily say, *ah,*

I am so swept up by the splendor,
on my ladder, edging the trim
along the crown molding, up where

the fumes concentrate. I am stroking
the paint onto every formerly white inch,
and of course I know *Semele* will end,

but it doesn't seem it ever has to:
this seemingly endless chain of glorious conclusions,

writhing stacked superb filigree
—let it open out endlessly,
let door after door be slid back

to reveal the next cadence,
the new phrasing, onward and on.

I am stilled now, atop my ladder,
leaning back onto the rungs, am the rapture
of denied closure, no need to go anywhere,

entirety forming and reasserting itself, an endless
—self-enfolding, self-devouring—

of which Handel constructs a model
in music's intricate apportionment
of minutes. And then there's barely a beat

of a pause before we move on to Haydn,
and I am nowhere near the end of my work.

from
TURTLE, SWAN
(1987)

TURTLE, SWAN

Because the road to our house
is a back road, meadowlands punctuated
by gravel quarry and lumberyard,
there are unexpected travelers
some nights on our way home from work.
Once, on the lawn of the Tool

and Die Company, a swan;
the word doesn't convey the shock
of the thing, white architecture
rippling like a pond's rain-pocked skin,
beak lifting to hiss at my approach.
Magisterial, set down in elegant authority,

he let us know exactly how close we might come.
After a week of long rains
that filled the marsh until it poured
across the road to make in low woods
a new heaven for toads,
a snapping turtle lumbered down the center

of the asphalt like an ambulatory helmet.
His long tail dragged, blunt head jutting out
of the lapidary prehistoric sleep of shell.
We'd have lifted him from the road
but thought he might bend his long neck back
to snap. I tried herding him; he rushed,

though we didn't think those blocky legs
could hurry—then ambled back
to the center of the road, a target
for kids who'd delight in the crush
of something slow with the look
of primeval invulnerability. He turned

the blunt spearpoint of his jaws,
puffing his undermouth like a bullfrog,
and snapped at your shoe,
vising a beakful of—thank God—
leather. You had to shake him loose. We left him
to his own devices, talked on the way home

of what must lead him to new marsh
or old home ground. The next day you saw,
one town over, remains of shell
in front of the little liquor store. I argued
it was too far from where we'd seen him,
too small to be his . . . though who could tell

what the day's heat might have taken
from his body. For days he became a stain,
a blotch that could have been merely
oil. I did not want to believe that
was what we saw alive in the firm center
of his authority and right

to walk the center of the road,
head up like a missionary moving certainly
into the country of his hopes.
In the movies in this small town
I stopped for popcorn while you went ahead
to claim seats. When I entered the cool dark

I saw straight couples everywhere,
no single silhouette who might be you.
I walked those two aisles too small
to lose anyone and thought of a book
I read in seventh grade, *Stranger Than Science*,
in which a man simply walked away,

at a picnic, and was,
in the act of striding forward
to examine a flower, gone.
By the time the previews ended
I was nearly in tears—then realized
the head of one-half the couple in the first row

was only your leather jacket propped in the seat
that would be mine. I don't think I remember
anything of the first half of the movie.
I don't know what happened to the swan. I read
every week of some man's lover showing
the first symptoms, the night sweat

or casual flu, and then the wasting begins
and the disappearance a day at a time.
I don't know what happened to the swan;
I don't know if the stain on the street
was our turtle or some other. I don't know
where these things we meet and know briefly,

as well as we can or they will let us,
go. I only know that I do not want you
—you with your white and muscular wings
that rise and ripple beneath or above me,
your magnificent neck, eyes the deep mottled autumnal colors
of polished tortoise—I do not want you ever to die.

CHARLIE HOWARD'S DESCENT

Between the bridge and the river
he falls through
a huge portion of night;
it is not as if falling

is something new. Over and over
he slipped into the gulf
between what he knew and how
he was known. What others wanted

opened like an abyss: the laughing
stock-clerks at the grocery, women
at the luncheonette amused by his gestures.
What could he do, live

with one hand tied
behind his back? So he began to fall
into the star-faced section
of night between the trestle

and the water because he could not meet
a little town's demands,
and his earrings shone and his wrists
were as limp as they were.

I imagine he took the insults in
and made of them a place to live;
we learn to use the names
because they are there,

familiar furniture: *faggot*
was the bed he slept in, hard
and white, but simple somehow,
queer something sharp

but finally useful, a tool,
all the jokes a chair,
stiff-backed to keep the spine straight,
a table, a lamp. And because

he's fallen for twenty-three years,
despite whatever awkwardness
his flailing arms and legs assume
he is beautiful

and like any good diver
has only an edge of fear
he transforms into grace.
Or else he is not afraid,

and in this way climbs back
up the ladder of his fall,
out of the river into the arms
of the three teenage boys

who hurled him from the edge—
really boys now, afraid,
their fathers' cars shivering behind them,
headlights on—and tells them

it's all right, that he knows
they didn't believe him
when he said he couldn't swim,
and blesses his killers

in the way that only the dead
can afford to forgive.

from
BETHLEHEM IN
BROAD DAYLIGHT
(1991)

SIX THOUSAND TERRA-COTTA MEN
AND HORSES

Some farmers digging a well
five kilometers outside of Xian
broke through into the tomb,
and corrosive daylight fell

onto the necks of the horses,
the men's knotted hair,
after their dynasties in the dark.
The rooms had been studded

with torches of seals' fat,
so these eyes could, even buried,
give back light. What did the Emperor expect
when the oiled strips of silk

were consumed, smoldering?
The guards were individuated by the sculptors
—whoever they may have been—
down to an idiosyncratic chin, the detail

of a frown. This one 192 centimeters tall,
this 186. "Life-size," the catalog says.
Were they portraits, each someone recognized
once, lively and exact? They ranked

in squadrons, self-contained, at rest.
Did the chamber smell of scorched fat still?
And to bury even horses, these animated faces
who look eager to step out onto the wide,

grassy fields outside of Xian.
Their breed is still raised in Quinghai;
the colors incinerated by daylight
must have made them less alien, less formal.

Muscular, monumental as coffins set on end,
they are patient and eager at once,
poised as if beginning the first step
of a purely ornamental journey,

sun on their backs, nothing at stake,
the provinces united years ago
under the Emperor's beautiful will,
which came to nothing, though his horses stared

into the dark for two thousand years,
good-natured, their faces open and uncomplicated.

ARARAT

Wrapped in gold foil, in the search
and shouting of Easter Sunday,
it was the ball of the princess,
it was Pharoah's body
sleeping its golden case.
At the foot of the picket fence,
in grass lank with the morning rain,
it was a Sunday school prize,
silver for second place, gold
for the triumphant little dome
of Ararat, and my sister
took me by the hand and led me
out onto the wide, wet lawn
and showed me to bend into the thick nests
of grass, into the darkest green.
Later I had to give it back,
in exchange for a prize,
though I would rather have kept the egg.
What might have coiled inside it?
Crocuses tight on their clock-springs,
a bird who'd sing himself into an angel
in the highest reaches of the garden,
the morning's flaming arrow?
Any small thing can save you.
Because the golden egg gleamed
in my basket once, though my childhood
became an immense sheet of darkening water
I was Noah, and I was his ark,
and there were two of every animal inside me.

ADONIS THEATRE

It must have seemed the apex of dreams,
the movie palace on Eighth Avenue
with its tiered chrome ticket booth,
Tibetan, the phantom blonde head

of the cashier floating
in its moon window. They'd outdone each other
all over the neighborhood, raising
these blunt pastiches of anywhere

we couldn't go: a pagoda, a future,
a Nepal. The avenue fed into the entry
with its glass cases of radiant stars,
their eyes dreamy and blown

just beyond human proportions to prepare us
for how enormous they would become inside,
after the fantastic ballroom of the lobby,
when the uniformed usher would show the way

to seats reserved for us in heaven.
I don't know when it closed,
or it ever shut down entirely,
but sometime—the forties?—

they stopped repainting the frescoes,
and when the plaster fell they merely
swept it away, and allowed
the gaps in the garlands of fruit

that decked the ceiling above the second balcony.
The screen shrunk to a soiled blank
where these smaller films began to unreel,
glorifying not the face but the body.

Or rather, bodies, ecstatic
and undifferentiated, as one film ends
and the next begins its brief and awkward exposition
before it reaches the essential matter

of flesh. No one pays much attention
to the screen. The viewers wander
in the steady, generous light washing back
up the long aisles toward the booth.

Perhaps we're hurt by becoming
beautiful in the dark, whether we watch
Douglas Fairbanks escaping from a dreamed,
suavely oriental city—think of these leaps

from the parapet, how he almost flies
from the grasp of whatever would limit him—
or the banal athletics of two or more men who were
and probably remain strangers. Perhaps

there's something cruel in the design
of the exquisite plaster box
built to frame the exotic
and call it desirable. When the show's over,

it is, whether it's the last frame
of Baghdad or the impossibly extended
come shot. And the solitary viewers,
the voyeurs and married men go home,

released from the swinging chrome doors
with their splendid reliefs
of the implements of artistry,
released into the streets as though washed

in something, marked with some temporary tattoo
that will wear away on the train ride home,
before anyone has time to punish them for it.
Something passing, even though the blood,

momentarily, has broken into flower
in the palace of limitless desire—
how could one ever be done with a god?
All its illusion conspires,

as it always has, to show us one another
in this light, whether we look to
or away from the screen.

THE DEATH OF ANTINOUS

When the beautiful young man drowned—
accidentally, swimming at dawn
in a current too swift for him,
or obedient to some cult
of total immersion that promised
the bather would come up divine,

mortality rinsed from him—
Hadrian placed his image everywhere,
a marble Antinous staring across
the public squares where a few dogs
always scuffled, planted
in every squalid little crossroad

at the farthest corners of the Empire.
What do we want in any body
but the world? And if the lover's
inimitable form was nowhere,
then he would find it everywhere,
though the boy became simply more dead

as the sculptors embodied him.
Wherever Hadrian might travel,
the beloved figure would be there
first: the turn of his shoulders,
the exact marble nipples,
the drowned face not really lost

to the Nile—which has no appetite,
merely takes in anything
without judgment of expectation—
but lost into its own multiplication,
an artifice rubbed with oils and acid
so that the skin might shine.

Which of these did I love?
Here is his hair, here his hair
again. Here the chiseled liquid waist
I hold because I cannot hold it.
If only one of you, he might have said
to any of the thousand marble boys anywhere,

would speak. Or the statues might have been enough,
the drowned boy blurred as much by memory
as by water, molded toward an essential,
remote ideal. Longing, of course,
become its own object, the way
that desire can make anything into a god.

TIARA

Peter died in a paper tiara
cut from a book of princess paper dolls;
he loved royalty, sashes

and jewels. *I don't know,*
he said, when he woke in the hospice,
I was watching the Bette Davis film festival

on Channel 57 and then—
At the wake, the tension broke
when someone guessed

the casket closed because
he was in there in a big wig
and heels, and someone said,

You know he's always late,
he probably isn't here yet—
he's still fixing his makeup.

And someone said he asked for it.
Asked for it—
when all he did was go down

into the salt tide
of wanting as much as he wanted,
giving himself over so drunk

or stoned it almost didn't matter who,
though they were beautiful,
stampeding into him in the simple,

ravishing music of their hurry.
I think heaven is perfect stasis
poised over the realms of desire,

where dreaming and waking men lie
on the grass while wet horses
roam among them, huge fragments

of the music we die into
in the body's paradise.
Sometimes we wake not knowing

how we came to lie here,
or who has crowned us with these temporary,
precious stones. And given

the world's perfectly turned shoulders,
the deep hollows blued by longing,
given the irreplaceable silk

of horses rippling in orchards,
fruit thundering and chiming down,
given the ordinary marvels of form

and gravity, what could he do,
what could any of us ever do
but ask for it?

from
MY ALEXANDRIA
(1993)

DEMOLITION

The intact façade's now almost black
in the rain; all day they've torn at the back
of the building, "the oldest concrete structure
in New England," the newspaper said. By afternoon
when the backhoe claw appears above
three stories of columns and cornices,

the crowd beneath their massed umbrellas cheer.
Suddenly the stairs seem to climb down themselves,
atomized plaster billowing: dust of 1907's
rooming house, this year's bakeshop and florist's,
the ghosts of their signs faint above the windows
lined, last week, with loaves and blooms.

We love disasters that have nothing to do
with us: the metal scoop seems shy, tentative,
a Japanese monster tilting its yellow head
and considering what to topple next. It's a weekday,
and those of us with the leisure to watch
are out of work, unemployable or academics,

joined by a thirst for watching something fall.
All summer, at loose ends, I've read biographies,
Wilde and Robert Lowell, and fallen asleep
over a fallen hero lurching down a Paris boulevard,
talking his way to dinner or a drink,
unable to forget the vain and stupid boy

he allowed to ruin him. And I dreamed
I was Lowell, in a manic flight of failing
and ruthless energy, and understood
how wrong I was with a passionate exactitude
which had to be like his. A month ago,
at Saint-Gaudens' house, we ran from a startling downpour

into coincidence: under a loggia built
for performances on the lawn
hulked Shaw's monument, splendid
in its plaster maquette, the ramrod-straight colonel
high above his black troops. We crouched on wet gravel
and waited out the squall; the hieratic woman

—a wingless angel?—floating horizontally
above the soldiers, her robe billowing like plaster dust,
seemed so far above us, another century's
allegorical décor, an afterthought
who'd never descend to the purely physical
soldiers, the nearly breathing bronze ranks crushed

into a terrible compression of perspective,
as if the world hurried them into the ditch.
"The unreadable," Wilde said, "is what occurs."
And when the brutish metal rears
above the wall of unglazed windows—
where, in a week, the kids will skateboard

in their lovely loops and spray
their indecipherable ideograms
across the parking lot—the single standing wall
seems Roman, momentarily, an aqueduct,
all that's left of something difficult
to understand now, something Oscar

and Bosie might have posed before, for a photograph.
Aqueducts and angels, here on Main,
seem merely souvenirs; the gaps
where the windows opened once
into transients' rooms are pure sky.
It's strange how much more beautiful

the sky is to us when it's framed
by these columned openings someone meant us
to take for stone. The enormous, articulate shovel
nudges the highest row of moldings
and the whole thing wavers as though we'd dreamed it,
our black classic, and it topples all at once.

THE WARE COLLECTION OF GLASS FLOWERS
AND FRUIT, HARVARD MUSEUM

Strange paradise, complete with worms,
monument of an obsessive will to fix forms;
every apricot or yellow spot's seen so closely,
in these blown blooms and fruit, that exactitude

is not quite imitation. Leaf and root,
the sweet flag's flaring bud already,
at the tip, blackened: it's hard to remember
these were ballooned and shaped by breath.

They're lovely because they seem
to decay: blue spots on bluer plums,
mold tarring a striped rose. I don't want to admire
the glassblower's academic replica,

his copies correct only to a single sense.
And why did a god so invested in permanence
choose so fragile a medium, the last material
he might expect to last? Better prose

to tell the forms of things, or illustration.
Though there's something seductive in this impossibility:
transparent color telling the live mottle of peach,
the blush or tint of crab, englobed,

gorgeous, edible. How else match that flush?
He's built a perfection out of hunger,
fused layer upon layer, swirled until
what can't be tasted, won't yield,

almost satisfies, an art
mouthed to the shape of how soft things are,
how good, before they disappear.

BROADWAY

Under Grand Central's tattered vault
   —maybe half a dozen electric stars still lit—
      one saxophone blew, and a sheer black scrim

billowed over some minor constellation
   under repair. Then, on Broadway, red wings
      in a storefront tableau, lustrous, the live macaws

preening, beaks opening and closing
   like those animated knives that unfold all night
      in jewelers' windows. For sale,

glass eyes turned out toward the rain,
   the birds lined up like the endless flowers
      and cheap gems, the makeshift tables

of secondhand magazines
   and shoes the hawkers eye
      while they shelter in the doorways of banks.

So many pockets and paper cups
   and hands reeled over the weight
      of that glittered pavement, and at 103rd

a woman reached to me across the wet roof
   of a stranger's car and said, *I'm Carlotta,*
      I'm hungry. She was only asking for change,

so I don't know why I took her hand,
   The rooftops were glowing above us,
      enormous, crystalline, a second city

lit from within. That night
a man on the downtown local stood up
and said, *My name is Ezekiel,*

*I am a poet, and my poem this evening is called
fall.* He stood up straight
to recite, a child reminded of his posture

by the gravity of his text, his hands
hidden in the pockets of his coat.
Love is protected, he said,

*the way leaves are packed in snow,
the rubies of fall. God is protecting
the jewel of love for us.*

He didn't ask for anything, but I gave him
the change left in my pocket,
and the man beside me, impulsive, moved,

gave Ezekiel his watch.
It wasn't an expensive watch,
I don't even know if it worked,

but the poet started, then walked away
as if so much good fortune
must be hurried away from,

before anyone realizes it's a mistake.
Carlotta, her stocking cap glazed
like feathers in the rain,

under the radiant towers, the floodlit ramparts,
must have wondered at my impulse to touch her,
which was like touching myself,

the way your own hand feels when you hold it
  because you want to feel contained.
    She said, *You get home safe now, you hear?*

In the same way Ezekiel turned back
  to the benevolent stranger.
    I will write a poem for you tomorrow,

he said. *The poem I will write will go like this:*
  Our ancestors are replenishing
    the jewel of love for us.

DAYS OF 1981

Cambridge Street, summer,
and a boy in a blue bandanna brought the bartender
flowers: delphiniums, splendid, blackened

in the dim room, though it was still afternoon, "tea
dance," in the heat of early July. Men in too-tight jeans
—none of them dancing—watched

the black women singing. Secret advocates of our hearts,
they urged us on as they broke apart
in painterly chaos on the video screen,

gowns and wigs, perfectly timed gestures
becoming bits of iridescent weather,
in the club's smoked atmosphere. The Supremes

—by then historical, lushly ascetic—then the endless
stream of women we loved, emblematic, reckless
in their attachments, or so the songs would have us think.

The man I met, slight and dark as Proust, a sultry flirt,
introduced himself because he liked my yellow shirt.
I don't remember who bought who drinks,

or why I liked him; I think it was simply
that I could. The heady rush of quickly
leaving together, late sun glaring over the Charles,

those last white sails blinding: it was so easy,
and strangely exhilarating, and free
as the women singing: a tidal, glimmering whirl

into which you could ease down, without thinking,
and simply be swept away. I was ready and waiting
to be swept. After the subway ride,

he knelt in front of me on the bleachers
in an empty suburban park, and I reached
for anything to hold onto, my head thrown back

to blue-black sky rinsed at the rim
with blazing city lights, then down to him:
relentless, dazzling, anyone. The smokestacks

and office towers loomed, a half-lit backdrop
beyond the baseball diamond. I didn't want him to ever stop,
and he left me breathless and unsatisfied.

He was a sculptor, and for weeks afterward I told myself
I loved him, because I'd met a man and wasn't sure
I could meet another—I'd never tried—

and because the next morning, starting
off to work, the last I saw of him, he gave me a heart,
ceramic, the marvel of a museum school show

his class had mounted. No one could guess
how he'd fired hollow clay entirely seamless
and kept it from exploding. I thought it beautiful, though

I was wrong about so much: him,
my prospects, the charm of the gift.
Out of context, it was a cool,

lumpish thing, earth-toned, lop-sided,
incapable of standing on its own. I propped
it up with books, then left it somewhere, eventually,

though I don't mind thinking of it now,
when I don't have the first idea where it's gone.
I called him more than twice.

If I knew where he was, even his last name,
(something French?) I might call again
to apologize for my naive

persistence, my lack of etiquette,
my ignorance of the austere code of tricks.
I didn't know then how to make love like that.

I thought of course we'd go on learning
the fit of chest to chest, curve to curve.
I didn't understand the ethos, the drama

of the search,
the studied approach to touch
as brief and recklessly enjambed

as the magic songs: *Give me just a little more
time, I'm so excited, I will survive.*
Nothing was promised, nothing sustained

or lethal offered. I wish I'd kept the heart.
Even the emblems of our own embarrassment
become acceptable to us, after a while,

evidence of someone we'd once have wished to erase:
a pottery heart,
an unrecaptured thing that might represent

the chancy exhilaration of a day, years ago
—*1981*—bleached sails on the Charles blowing,
the blue-black women in their rapture on the screen,

their perfected longing and release.
The astonishing flowers, seething
a blue I could barely see.

HUMAN FIGURES

On the Number 15 bus on Potrero Hill,
San Francisco, a morning of clouds shifting
like ripples on silk, a black man
a few seats in front of me covers his lap

with Chinese newspapers and smooths
the rumpled sheets across his thighs
over and over. I think he's hiding
something beneath them, himself perhaps,

until looking directly out the windows
with their clouds he begins to tear
the sheets of newspaper in half
and rolls the delicate black moss

of calligraphy into a cone, twists it
into something intricate between his broad hands,
something he doesn't want anyone to see.
Then he places whatever he's made

on the seat beside him and covers it,
covertly, another sheet of news,
and tears and rolls, furiously, as though
he can't make one thing and leave it alone.

I think he's seen me watching,
and I try not to look as he keeps
rolling faster, till we reach a stop
and a quick gust of wind from the door

lifts the paper veil just enough to reveal
what he's made. Once, in Boston,
a vagrant lay on one of the long stone benches
by the Public Library, bleeding.

I don't know what had happened;
a little crescent of people clustered,
waiting for the ambulance
to work its way through traffic.

I didn't want to be like them,
didn't want to look, and a sheet of newspaper,
a page of the *Globe* ripping down Boylston,
skittered across the red slick of him and tumbled

toward me, the stain already drying
on four columns of news. Soon
it wouldn't even be recognizable,
the blood in its morning edition

blowing across my shoes. Suppose the ambulance
hadn't come and he'd kept on bleeding,
a stain larger than his own body
darkening the cement and all the paper

blown along those windy steps?
Imagine he'd kept on publishing himself
until his outline were larger than anything
the police could chalk, uncontained,

the shapeless bulletin of the news you can't buy,
though you can't help but read it.
And the man in San Francisco twists his papers
into dolls, tiny human forms—

like ginseng roots floating
in Chinatown windows, long limbs streaming out
behind them—figures molded
into something intimate, something to hide.

ALMOST BLUE

Chet Baker, 1929–1988

If Hart Crane played trumpet
he'd sound like you, your horn's dark city

miraculous and broken over and over,
scale-shimmered, every harbor-flung hour

and salt-span of cabled longing,
every waterfront, the night-lovers' rendezvous.

This is the entrance
to the city of you, sleep's hellgate,

and two weeks before the casual relinquishment
of your hold—light needling

on the canal's gleaming haze
and the buds blaring like horns—

two weeks before the end, Chet,
and you're playing like anything,

singing *stay little valentine*
stay

and taking so long there are worlds sinking
between the notes, this exhalation

no longer a voice but a rush of air,
brutal, from the tunnels under the river,

the barges' late whistles you only hear
when the traffic's stilled

by snow, a city hushed and
distilled into one rush of breath,

yours, into the microphone
and the ear of that girl

in the leopard-print scarf,
one long kiss begun on the highway

and carried on dangerously,
the Thunderbird veering

on the coast road: glamor
of a perfectly splayed fender,

dazzling lipstick, a little pearl of junk,
some stretch of road breathless

and traveled into . . . Whoever she is
she's the other coast of you,

and just beyond the bridge the city's
long amalgam of ardor and indifference

is lit like a votive
then blown out. Too many rooms unrented

in this residential hotel,
and you don't want to know

why they're making that noise in the hall;
you're going to wake up in any one of the

how many ten thousand
locations of trouble and longing

going out of business forever everything must go
wake up and start wanting.

It's so much better when you don't want:
nothing falls then, nothing lost

but sleep and who wanted that
in the pearl this suspended world is,

in the warm suspension and glaze
of this song everything stays up

almost forever in the long
glide sung into the vein,

one note held almost impossibly
almost blue and the lyric takes so long

to open, a little blood
blooming: *there's no love song finer*

but how strange the change
from major to minor

every time
we say goodbye

and you leaning into that warm
haze from the window, Amsterdam,

late afternoon glimmer
a blur of buds

breathing in the lindens
and you let go and why not

ESTA NOCHE

In a dress with a black tulip's sheen
    la fabulosa Lola enters, late, mounts the stairs
to the plywood platform, and begs whoever runs
    the wobbling spot to turn the lights down

to something flattering. When they halo her
    with a petal-toned gel, she sets to haranguing,
shifting in and out of two languages like gowns
    or genders to please have a little respect

for the girls, flashing the one entrancing
    and unavoidable gap in the center of her upper teeth.
And when the cellophane drop goes black,
    a new spot coronas her in a wig

fit for the end of a century,
    and she tosses back her hair—risky gesture—
and raises her arms like a widow in a blood tragedy,
    all will and black lace, and lip-synchs "You and Me

Against the World." She's a man
    you wouldn't look twice at in street clothes,
two hundred pounds of hard living, the gap in her smile
    sadly narrative—but she's a monument,

in the mysterious permission of the dress.
    This is Esta Noche, a Latin drag bar in the Mission,
its black door a gap in the face
    of a battered wall. All over the neighborhood

storefront windows show all night
   shrined hats and gloves, wedding dresses,
First Communion's frothing lace:
   gowns of perfection and commencement,

fixed promises glowing. In the dress
   the color of the spaces between streetlamps
Lola stands unassailable, the dress
   in which she is in the largest sense

fabulous: a lesson, a criticism and colossus
   of gender, all fire and irony. Her spine's
perfectly erect, only her fluid hands moving
   and her head turned slightly to one side.

She hosts the pageant, Wednesdays and Saturdays,
   and men come in from the streets, the trains
and the repair shops, lean together to rank
   the artifice of the awkward or lovely

Lola welcomes onto her stage: Victoria, Elena,
   Francie, lamé pumps and stockings and always
the rippling night pulled down over broad shoulders
   and flounced around the hips, liquid,

the black silk of esta noche
   proving that perfection and beauty are so alien
they almost never touch. Tonight, she says,
   put it on. The costume is license

and calling. She says you could wear the whole damn
   black sky and all its spangles. It's the only night
we have to stand on. Put it on,
   it's the only thing we have to wear.

FOG

The crested iris by the front gate waves
its blue flags three days, exactly,

then they vanish. The peony buds'
tight wrappings are edged crimson;

when they open, a little blood-color
will ruffle at the heart of the flounced,

unbelievable white. Three weeks after the test,
the vial filled from the crook

of my elbow, I'm seeing blood everywhere:
a casual nick from the garden shears,

a shaving cut and I feel the physical rush
of the welling up, the wine-fountain

dark as Siberian iris. The thin green porcelain
teacup, our homemade Ouija's planchette,

rocks and wobbles every night, spins
and spells. It seems a cloud of spirits

numerous as lilac panicles vie for occupancy—
children grabbing for the telephone,

happy to talk to someone who isn't dead yet?
Everyone wants to speak at once, or at least

these random words appear, incongruous
and exactly spelled: *energy, immunity, kiss.*

Then: M. *has immunity. W. has.*
And that was all. One character, Frank,

distinguishes himself: a boy who lived
in our house in the thirties, loved dogs

and gangster movies, longs for a body,
says he can watch us through the television,

asks us to stand before the screen
and kiss. *God in garden*, he says.

Sitting out on the back porch at twilight,
I'm almost convinced. In this geometry

of paths and raised beds, the green shadows
of delphinium, there's an unseen rustling:

some secret amplitude
seems to open in this orderly space.

Maybe because it contains so much dying,
all these tulip petals thinning

at the base until any wind takes them.
I doubt anyone else would see that, looking in,

and then I realize my garden has no outside, only *is*
subjectively. As blood is utterly without

an outside, can't be seen except out of context,
the wrong color in alien air, no longer itself.

Though it submits to test, two,
to be exact, each done three times,

though not for me, since at their first entry
into my disembodied blood

there was nothing at home there.
For you they entered the blood garden over

and over, like knocking at a door
because you know someone's home. Three times

the Elisa Test, three the Western Blot,
and then the incoherent message. We're

the public health care worker's
nine o'clock appointment,

she is a phantom hand who forms
the letters of your name, and the word

that begins with P. I'd lie out
and wait for the god if it weren't

so cold, the blue moon huge
and disruptive above the flowering crab's

foaming collapse. The spirits say Fog
when they can't speak clearly

and the letters collide; sometimes
for them there's nothing outside the mist

of their dying. Planchette,
peony, I would think of anything

not to say the word. Maybe the blood
in the flower is a god's. Kiss me,

in front of the screen, please,
the dead are watching.

They haven't had enough yet.
Every new bloom is falling apart.

I would say anything else
in the world, any other word.

NIGHT FERRY

We're launched into the darkness,
half a load of late passengers
   gliding onto the indefinite
      black surface, a few lights vague

and shimmering on the island shore.
Behind us, between the landing's twin flanks
   (wooden pylons strapped with old tires),
      the docklights shatter in our twin,

folding wakes, their colors
on the roughened surface combed
   like the patterns of Italian bookpaper,
      lustrous and promising. The narrative

of the ferry begins and ends brilliantly,
and its text is this moving out
   into what is soon before us
      and behind: the night going forward,

sentence by sentence, as if on faith,
into whatever takes place.
   It's strange how we say things *take place*,
      as if occurrence were a location—

the dark between two shores,
for instance, where for a little while
   we're on no solid ground. Twelve minutes,
      precisely, the night ferry hurries

across the lake. And what happens
is always the body of water,
    its skin like the wrong side of satin.
        I love to stand like this,

    where the prow pushes blunt into the future,
knowing, more than seeing, how
    the surface rushes and doesn't even break
        but simply slides under us.

    Lake melds into shoreline,
one continuous black moire;
    the boatmen follow the one course they know
        toward a dock nearly the mirror

    of the first, mercury lamps vaporing
over the few late birds
    attending the pier. Even the bored men
        at the landing, who wave

    their flashlights for the last travelers,
steering us toward the road, will seem
    the engineers of our welcome,
        their red-sheathed lights marking

    the completion of our, or anyone's, crossing.
Twelve dark minutes. Love,
    we are between worlds, between
        unfathomed water and I don't know how much

    light-flecked black sky, the fogged circles
of island lamps. I am almost not afraid
    on this good boat, breathing its good smell
        of grease and kerosene,

warm wind rising up the stairwell
from the engine's serious study.
   There's no beautiful binding
     for this story, only the temporary,

   liquid endpapers of the hurried water,
shot with random color. But in the gliding forward's
   a scent so quick and startling
     it might as well be blowing

   off the stars. Now, just before we arrive,
the wind carries a signal and a comfort,
   lovely, though not really meant for us:
     woodsmoke risen from the chilly shore.

NO

The children have brought their wood turtle
into the dining hall
because they want us to feel

the power they have
when they hold a house
in their own hands, want us to feel

alien lacquer and the little thrill
that he might, like God, show his face.
He's the color of ruined wallpaper,

of cognac, and he's closed,
pulled in as though he'll never come out;
nothing shows but the plummy leather

of the legs, his claws resembling clusters
of diminutive raspberries.
They know he makes night

anytime he wants, so perhaps
he feels at the center of everything,
as they do. His age,

greater than that of anyone
around the table, is a room
from which they are excluded,

though they don't mind,
since they can carry this perfect
building anywhere. They love

that he might poke out
his old, old face, but doesn't.
I think the children smell unopened,

like unlit candles, as they heft him
around the table, praise his secrecy,
holding to each adult face

his prayer,
the single word of the shell,
which is no.

BRILLIANCE

Maggie's taking care of a man
who's dying; he's attended to everything,
said goodbye to his parents,

paid off his credit card.
She says *Why don't you just*
run it up to the limit?

but he wants everything
squared away, no balance owed,
though he misses the pets

he's already found a home for
—he can't be around dogs or cats,
too much risk. He says,

I can't have anything.
She says, *A bowl of goldfish?*
He says he doesn't want to start

with anything and then describes
the kind he'd maybe like,
how their tails would fan

to a gold flaring. They talk
about hot jewel tones,
gold lacquer, say maybe

they'll go pick some out
though he can't go much of anywhere and then
abruptly he says *I can't love*

anything I can't finish.
He says it like he's had enough
of the whole scintillant world,

though what he means is
he'll never be satisfied and therefore
has established this discipline,

a kind of severe rehearsal.
That's where they leave it,
him looking out the window,

her knitting as she does because
she needs to do something.
Later he leaves a message:

Yes to the bowl of goldfish.
Meaning: let me go, if I have to,
in brilliance. In a story I read,

a Zen master who'd perfected
his detachment from the things of the world
remembered, at the moment of dying,

a deer he used to feed in the park,
and wondered who might care for it,
and at that instant was reborn

in the stunned flesh of a fawn.
So, Maggie's friend—
is he going out

into the last loved object
of his attention?
Fanning the veined translucence

of an opulent tail,
undulant in some uncapturable curve,
is he bronze chrysanthemums,

copper leaf, hurried darting,
doubloons, icon-colored fins
troubling the water?

WITH ANIMALS

Wet grass, headlights streaking morning fog,
    and three deer sudden in my friends' driveway:

lithe buck leaping in seconds
    onto the stone embankment, flash of doe following,

then the slim-hipped adolescent, mossy antlers
    sprouting . . . So much hurrying life in them,

glancing off the human world,
    like the herons I used to watch in the country,

the morning's steel-feathered news
    poised on the single lip of rock

cresting the river, upright, each a yard
    of oystery shantung, fog-toned, lyrical

and awkward at once. In air they were fire,
    that easy, over the railroad shacks where dawn

broke the pearl veil of acres and acres
    of fog. Then they were gone for days, and gone

all winter. From those steep-raked hills
    so many bells rang, and nights when it snowed

it was as if the tolling were hung
    in the air over town, the chiming

actually vibrating through each snowflake
    until the bells would reverberate

against the granite hillside
   and the frozen surface of the river

whose banks had grown together, all November,
   as ice moved up from the cataract,

through which the bells rang also,
   ice doubling them again.

The colder the night the more perfectly the air
   itself seemed to ring, the whole storm

swirling around us. My dog would stand
   caught in that sound, absolutely still,

while the ringing passed through his solid
   year-old body and he would look up,

head cocked slightly, as if for an explanation.
   That winter, just to feel I owned something,

I drove once a week to our cabin in the woods.
   Something chimed from the thickets one January morning

like a bird continuing the hammer of its call
   over and over without stirring from its branch,

and I followed the sound until I could see
   from the road—I don't want to tell this—

what looked like a nest, a cluster of necks
   moving back and forth above the snow.

And I crouched into the brush
   and saw what called: four paws thrust up

from a hole the heat of a body had melted;
    it must have been lying there all night,

running on its back. The hole was wider,
    close to the soil, and the animal's face

was hidden by snow. I thought, *It's a fox,*
    don't touch it, I thought, *touch it*. At first

I covered its face, as if that would help it die,
    but I couldn't do it, I scraped the snow away,

all of it, from its face: someone's
    fox-colored housedog, a dustcloth of a dog.

And feeling half-foolish and half entirely real
    I said *You can go if you want to,*

it's all right if you want to go.
    The dog never even looked at me, the dog

kept running almost mechanically, on its back
    in the stained nest, all four paws moving

in that pointless version of flight, nodding
    its head from side to side and making the little

choked sound, at exactly the same interval.
    That was what it could do. I didn't know

it had been shot in the head, as country people
    will do, when an animal has outlived its usefulness;

the man or boy with the rifle hadn't cared
    to make sure it was dead. It wasn't dead.

It wanted even a life reduced to this
    twitching repetition, no matter how diminished,

how brutal, how wrong. Something which was
    and was not the dog wanted to continue,

something entirely dependent upon that body
    which was already beginning to be rimed

with ice. Something cleaves to form
    until the last minute, past it,

and though the vet's needle was an act
    of mercy, the life needed to continue,

the life was larger than cruelty,
    the life denied the obliterating gesture

where only kindness had been expected.
    Even with one eye shot away and the brain spasming

the life takes it in and says *more*,
    just as it takes in the quick jab of the needle

and the flooding darkness. The life doesn't care.
    The life only wants, the fugitive life.

BILL'S STORY

When my sister came back from Africa,
we didn't know at first how everything
had changed. After a while Annie
bought men's and boys' clothes in all sizes,
and filled her closets with little
or huge things she could never wear.

Then she took to buying out
theatrical shops, rental places on the skids,
sweeping in and saying, *I'll take everything.*
Dementia was the first sign of something
we didn't even have a name for,
in 1978. She was just becoming stranger

—all those clothes, the way she'd dress me up
when I came to visit. It was like we could go back
to playing together again, and get it right.
She was a performance artist, and she did
her best work then, taking the clothes to clubs,
talking, putting them all on, talking.

It was years before she was in the hospital,
and my mother needed something
to hold onto, some way to be helpful,
so she read a book called *Deathing*:
(a cheap, ugly verb if ever I heard one)
and took its advice to heart;

she'd sit by the bed and say, Annie,
look for the light, look for the light.
It was plain that Anne did not wish
to be distracted by these instructions;
she came to, though she was nearly gone then,
and looked at our mother with what was almost certainly

annoyance. *It's a white light,*
Mom said, and this struck me
as incredibly presumptuous, as if the light
we'd all go into would be just the same.
Maybe she wanted to give herself up
to indigo, or red. If we can barely even speak

to each other, living so separately,
how can we all die the same?
I used to take the train to the hospital,
and sometimes the only empty seats
would be the ones that face backward.
I'd sit there and watch where I'd been

waver and blur out, and finally
I liked it, seeing what you've left
get more beautiful, less specific.
Maybe her light was all that gabardine
and flannel, khaki and navy
and silks and stripes. If you take everything,

you've got to let everything go. Dying
must take more attention than I ever imagined.
Just when she'd compose herself
and seem fixed on the work before her,
Mother would fret, trying to help
just one more time: *Look for the light,*

until I took her arm
and told her wherever I was in the world
I would come back, no matter how difficult
it was to reach her, if I heard her calling.
Shut up, mother, I said, and Annie died.

CHANTEUSE

Prendergast painted the Public Garden;
remembered, even at a little distance,
the city takes on his ravishing tones.

Jots of color resolve: massed parasols
above a glimmering pond, the transit
of almost translucent swans. Brilliant bits

—jewels? slices of sugared fruit?—bloom
into a clutch of skirts on the bridge
above the summer boaters. His city's essence:

all the hues of chintzes or makeup
or Italian ices, all the sheen artifice
is capable of. Our city's lavish paintbox.

Name the colors: light turning to rose,
a suspended glow, late afternoons,
in the air above the avenues,

as if the houses themselves were remembering,
their brick-tinted memory a warm haze
above the taxis and the homebound cars.

Almost the color of the glow, evenings,
at the end of April, when one lamppost
positioned exactly right, on Marlboro Street,

would shine through the unfurled petals
of a blossoming magnolia, marbling
a corner mailbox, an iron gate,

a tract of sidewalk—light stained by the skin
of flowers, the shadows of bloom. I loved
that city, the two of us traversing

that light. Name the colors: frothing pink
evidence of tulips beheaded in the Garden,
patinated rainstreaked green

of Dover Station's backstreet pagoda
rusting over the moon windows
of the Premier Diner, the surplus clothing store

of Harry the Greek—the Geek, everyone called him—
his windows painted over with the prices
of socks and trousers. What was our city

but wonderful detail? A scaffolding's
wrought-iron tiara, evening's violet smolder
over the avenue's noise and happy taxis.

Lit windows—possible futures
with their parchment glow, intimate interiors—
and then the brilliant red snow

of firecracker wrappings, Chinese New Year's
scatter of bright applause. Hammered copper
carp rising in a tank; beancakes in the baker's

window glazed in sugar water. A tangle
of crated squid. Flares, sparks shaking
the avenue awake, the tumbling fiery bolts

of blazing silk. Name the color, the one
you've been saving, memory's glimmering
spotlight and sequin: once, upstairs

in a nearly empty room over a crowded bar,
a beautiful black drag queen—perched
on the edge of the piano, under a blue spot,

her legs crossed in front of her
so that the straps of her sparkling ankle shoes
glimmered—sang only to us. The song

was Rodgers and Hart—*My romance*
doesn't have to have a moon in the sky—
and she was perfect. The piano's slow unfolding,

her smoke-burnished, entirely believable voice,
the sequins on her silver bolero
shimmering ice blue. Cavafy ends a poem

of regret and desire—
memory's erotics, his ashen atmosphere—
by going out onto a balcony

to change my thoughts at least
by seeing something of this city I love,
a little movement in the streets,

in the shops. That was all it took
to console him, some token of Alexandria's
anarchic life. How did it go on without him,

the city he'd transformed into feeling?
Hadn't he made it entirely
into himself? *High windy blue*, I wrote,

in one of those old notebooks one never
really reads again, *burning over the balconies.*
Whose city was it, Prendergast's,

Cavafy's, ours, the rapt singer
who caught us in the glory
of her artifice? One Christmas,

when the day broke every record
for warmth, we pried open our long-shut windows
above Beacon Street and the wind pouring

into that high-ceilinged room
swept every flake of paper snow
from the tree. We were awash in

a studio-sized blizzard, snow
on your sleeves and hair, and anything
that divided us then was bridged

by the sudden graceful shock
of being inside the warmest storm.
That is how I would describe her voice,

her lyric that becomes, now, my city:
torch, invitation, accomplishment. *My romance
doesn't need a blue lagoon standing by* . . .

As she invented herself, memory revises
and restores her, and the moment
she sang. I think we were perfected,

when we became her audience,
and maybe from that moment on
it didn't matter so much exactly

what would become of us.
I would say she was memory,
and we were restored by

the radiance of her illusion,
her consummate attention to detail,
—name the colors—her song: my Alexandria,

my romance, my magnolia
distilling lamplight, my backlit glory
of the wig shops, my haze

and glow, my torch, my skyrocket,
my city, my false,
my splendid chanteuse.

DIFFERENCE

The jellyfish
float in the bay shallows
like schools of clouds,

a dozen identical—is it right
to call them creatures,
these elaborate sacks

of nothing? All they seem
is shape, and shifting,
and though a whole troop

of undulant cousins
go about their business
within a single wave's span,

every one does something unlike:
this one a balloon
open on both ends

but swollen to its full expanse,
this one a breathing heart,
this a pulsing flower.

This one a rolled condom,
or a plastic purse swallowing itself,
that one a Tiffany shade,

this a troubled parasol.
This submarine opera's
all subterfuge and disguise,

its plot a fabulous tangle
of hiding and recognition:
nothing but trope,

nothing but something
forming itself into figures
then refiguring,

sheer ectoplasm
recognizable only as the stuff
of metaphor. What can words do

but link what we know
to what we don't,
and so form a shape?

Which shrinks or swells,
configures or collapses, blooms
even as it is described

into some unlikely
marine chiffon:
a gown for Isadora?

Nothing but style.
What binds
one shape to another

also sets them apart
—but what's lovelier
than the shapeshifting

transparence of *like* and *as*:
clear, undulant words?
We look at alien grace,

unfettered
by any determined form,
and we say: balloon, flower,

heart, condom, opera,
lampshade, parasol, ballet.
Hear how the mouth,

so full
of longing for the world,
changes its shape?

THE ADVENT CALENDARS

These were our first instruction
    in the power of the unopened.
They're lined up tonight
    edge to edge, a city of tiny windows

behind this small town shop's
    breath-steamed glass: frosty barns,
Bavarian villages, diluted Breughels
    where children sled on the slope

above the bridge, an owl nests
    in the high window of an attic.
Lamps in every kitchen.
    First you must find *One*,

the hidden world's premiere,
    a door which always gives onto
something minor. Then come days
    of incidental scenes, patient animals,

the entre'acte of miracle.
    Eventually—*Twelve*, say—
there's perhaps a shepherd boy
    washing down the stable floor,

a milkmaid bent over the earth's
    whitest treasure. Number after number
prolongs anticipation: *Sixteen*,
    an out-of-season dove carrying

a wisp of straw, quarried
     from what bank of snow; *Twenty-one*,
a kitten who's upset a saucer
     set out on the chilly flagstones.

About the final miracle,
     there's little surprise,
once you've seen it; you don't need
     to believe the story about space

pouring itself into the form
     of a god, the glory in the barn.
It's the promise that matters,
     twenty-five portals

incomplete until they're opened
     but then incomplete still,
since their charm lay in concealment.
     Moments from now we'll walk

our street's corridor of lit
     and darkened houses,
the exhaust-dimmed façades
     brightened by storm, interiors revealed

a window at a time, if at all.
     Nights like this
our town grows smaller,
     compressed under the freighted weather,

suspended white cargo sifting
     equally all night onto roofs
and lilacs, fence posts and streets.
     The shook heart of the paperweight,

the glass village falling forever
  through the steady arms
of the snow, which touch us,
  each pair, just once,

then let us go. Each particular's
  erased, exact form abstracted
into shape, the world gone
  general, unmoored, white.

Is God also in the absence
  of detail? The unlit spaces
between houses are thick with snow,
  but here and there a window's glow

illumines a steady shaft of falling,
  one perfect rhythm of hesitation:
the snow is an old, old story,
  in no hurry to be told.

Half the windows are open,
  half the windows closed.
There is no single location of miracle.

LAMENT-HEAVEN

What hazed around the branches
    late in March was white at first,
        as if a young tree's ghost

were blazing in the woods,
    a fluttering around the limbs
        like shredded sleeves. A week later,

green fountaining,
    frothing champagne;
        against the dark of evergreen,

that skyrocket shimmer. I think
    this is how our deaths would look,
        seen from a great distance,

if we could stand that far
    from ourselves: the way birch leaves
        signal and flash, candling

into green then winking out.
    You've seen lights along the shore
        move forward and recede,

not knowing if any single one were house
    or buoy, lamp or reflection:
        all one fabric. If death's like that,

if we are continuous,
    rippling from nothing into being,
        then why can't we let ourselves go

into the world's glimmering story?
   Who can become lost in a narrative,
      if all he can think of is the end?

Only lights in a lapping harbor—
   nothing to fear—rising again,
      going out. No,

faster than that

   ◆ ◆ ◆

like the carnival we saw one night,
   late, off the freeway on the South Shore,
      countless circuits of lightbulbs

hazing through thickening spring fog,
   the Ferris wheel's phosphorescent roulette
      fog-haloed, blazing.

Then letters blinking on—
   G-H-O-S-T—
      and the linked cursive of *train*:

a funhouse locomotive of spirits,
   passengers on the white air?
      Our guiding spirit,

spelling out his name and intention
   through the Ouija's rainbowed alphabet,
      isn't much help. Though death's

his single subject,
   he insists there is none,
      or rather that what awaits us is "home,"

something he'll say little about.
   What does he mean—
      the cloudy parlors of heaven

or the insubstantial stuff of earth:
   an amusement park alien in its glitter,
      the mud-fragrant woods, soaked,

tonight, in spring rain,
   warm and unlikely?
      He won't answer.

He says death is peace.
   I don't believe a word he spells;
      I don't believe the lamenting

stops at the borders of this world
   or any other. Why give a ghost letters
      and the twin poles of yes and no;

isn't everything so shadowed
   by its own brevity
      we can barely tell the thing

from its elegy? Strip something
   of its mortality, and how do you know
      what's left to see?

   ◆   ◆   ◆

In Sing Sing, on a chapel bulletin board,
   I read a sign someone spent hours lettering,
      the careful tattoo-on-paper

of a man with all the time
  in the world to make his point,
    text ringed around a Maltese cross:

God's not dead, I can 'feel' him
  all over me. In those miles of corridors
    men move from lock

to lock like canal water,
  each segment of hallway filling
    until the sluice gates open

and they pour into the next hall,
  so much black and blue water
    hurrying toward the shabby visitors' trailer.

My friend there says
  it's hard for him to write
    because so many men narrate

day and night the endless
  distracting monologues that keep them
    real: I am here,

doing this. I don't know
  how you could feel anything
    on your skin in there—

blows maybe, but not divinity.
  It's quiet here, I'm free to walk
    anywhere I want and nothing's touching me

that I'm certain I'd call endless,
  though I'd like to tell whoever inked
    that sign the truth, how last week

I felt this—godliness?—
    around me, in the enormous church
        in Copley Square, under the gold-ribbed vault

pierced by figured windows.
    A girl, twelve maybe, was playing the violin,
        —rapturously, though I suppose for her

it was not trance but discipline
    that made the music gather and then tumble
        like water collecting in a fountain,

all hesitation and sudden release.
    The organist who accompanied
        would stop her, from time to time,

and together they'd repeat a phrase,
    and then the music would seem to fall forward,
        tumbling snowmelt breaking loose

from the hidden place
    where it had been contained.
        She was a black girl,

with large round glasses which she pushed
    closer to her eyes each time she paused.
        I would have lived in that music,

or rather it was as if I had been once
    the cautious and splendid cascade from the violin.
        It was the sound that movement

through experience would make,
    if we could stand far enough away
        to hear it: lovely, and unconsoling,

each phrase played out
    into a dense thicket of variations,
        into its web of meanings, lifted

and reconsidered, articulated
    into exhaustion, hurried and then stilled,
        a crowd of wings. I can't remember

even the melody, which doesn't matter;
    there's nothing to hold
        but the memory of the sensation

of such moments, cancelling out
    the whine of the self
        that doesn't want to be ground down,

answering the little human cry
    at the heart of the elegy,
        Oh why aren't I what I wanted to be,

exempt from history?
    The music mounts up,
        assembles its architecture

larger than any of us
    and doesn't need you to continue.
        Do you understand me?

I heard it, the music
    that could not go on without us,
        and I was inconsolable.

from
ATLANTIS
(1995)

DESCRIPTION

My salt marsh
—mine, I call it, because
these day-hammered fields

of dazzled horizontals
undulate, summers,
inside me and out—

how can I say what it is?
Sea lavender shivers
over the tidewater steel.

A million minnows ally
with their million shadows
(lucky we'll never need

to know whose is whose).
The bud of storm loosens:
watered paint poured

dark blue onto the edge
of the page. Haloed grasses,
gilt shadow-edged body of dune . . .

I could go on like this.
I love the language
of the day's ten thousand aspects,

the creases and flecks
in the map, these
brilliant gouaches.

But I'm not so sure it's true,
what I was taught, that through
the particular's the way

to the universal:
what I need to tell is
swell and curve, shift

and blur of boundary,
tremble and spilling over,
a heady purity distilled

from detail. A metaphor, then:
in this tourist town,
the retail legions purvey

the far-flung world's
bangles: brilliance of Nepal
and Mozambique, any place

where cheap labor braids
or burnishes or hammers
found stuff into jewelry's

lush grammar,
a whole vocabulary
of ornament: copper and lacquer,

shells and seeds from backwaters
with fragrant names, millefiori
milled into African beads, Mexican abalone,

camel bone and tin, cinnabar
and verdigris, silver,
black onyx, coral,

gold: one vast conjugation
of the verb
to shine.

And that
is the marsh essence—
all the hoarded riches

of the world held
and rivering, a gleam
awakened and doubled

by water, flashing
off the bowing of the grass.
Jewelry, tides, language:

things that shine.
What is description, after all,
but encoded desire?

And if we say
the marsh, if we forge
terms for it, then isn't it

contained in us,
a little,
the brightness?

A GREEN CRAB'S SHELL

Not, exactly, green:
closer to bronze
preserved in kind brine,

something retrieved
from a Greco-Roman wreck,
patinated and oddly

muscular. We cannot
know what his fantastic
legs were like—

though evidence
suggests eight
complexly folded

scuttling works
of armament, crowned
by the foreclaws'

gesture of menace
and power. A gull's
gobbled the center,

leaving this chamber
—size of a demitasse—
open to reveal

a shocking, Giotto blue.
Though it smells
of seaweed and ruin,

this little traveling case
comes with such lavish lining!
Imagine breathing

surrounded by
the brilliant rinse
of summer's firmament.

What color is
the underside of skin?
Not so bad, to die,

if we could be opened
into this—
if the smallest chambers

of ourselves,
similarly,
revealed some sky.

A DISPLAY OF MACKEREL

They lie in parallel rows,
on ice, head to tail,
each a foot of luminosity

barred with black bands,
which divide the scales'
radiant sections

like seams of lead
in a Tiffany window.
Iridescent, watery

prismatics: think abalone,
the wildly rainbowed
mirror of a soapbubble sphere,

think sun on gasoline.
Splendor, and splendor,
and not a one in any way

distinguished from the other
—nothing about them
of individuality. Instead

they're *all* exact expressions
of the one soul,
each a perfect fulfilment

of heaven's template,
mackerel essence. As if,
after a lifetime arriving

at this enameling, the jeweler's
made uncountable examples,
each as intricate

in its oily fabulation
as the one before.
Suppose we could iridesce,

like these, and lose ourselves
entirely in the universe.
of shimmer—would you want

to be yourself only,
unduplicatable, doomed
to be lost? They'd prefer,

plainly, to be flashing participants,
multitudinous. Even now
they seem to be bolting

forward, heedless of stasis.
They don't care they're dead
and nearly frozen,

just as, presumably,
they didn't care that they were living:
all, all for all,

the rainbowed school
and its acres of brilliant classrooms,
in which no verb is singular,

or every one is. How happy they seem,
even on ice, to be together, selfless,
which is the price of gleaming.

ATLANTIS

1. Faith

                "I've been having these
awful dreams, each a little different,
though the core's the same—

we're walking in a field,
Wally and Arden and I, a stretch of grass
with a highway running beside it,

or a path in the woods that opens
onto a road. Everything's fine,
then the dog sprints ahead of us,

excited; we're calling but
he's racing down a scent and doesn't hear us,
and that's when he goes

onto the highway. I don't want to describe it.
Sometimes it's brutal and over,
and others he's struck and takes off

so we don't know where he is
or how bad. This wakes me
every night now, and I stay awake;

I'm afraid if I sleep I'll go back
into the dream. It's been six months,
almost exactly, since the doctor wrote

not even a real word
but an acronym, a vacant
four-letter cipher

that draws meanings into itself,
reconstitutes the world.
We tried to say it was just

a word; we tried to admit
it had power and thus to nullify it
by means of our acknowledgment.

I know the current wisdom:
bright hope, the power of wishing you're well.
He's just so tired, though nothing

shows in any tests, Nothing,
the doctor says, detectable;
the doctor doesn't hear what I do,

that trickling, steadily rising nothing
that makes him sleep all day,
vanish into fever's tranced afternoons,

and I swear sometimes
when I put my head to his chest
I can hear the virus humming

like a refrigerator.
Which is what makes me think
you can take your positive attitude

and go straight to hell.
We don't have a future,
we have a dog.

Soul without speech,
sheer, tireless faith,
he is that-which-goes-forward,

black muzzle, black paws
scouting what's ahead;
he is where we'll be hit first,

he's the part of us
that's going to get it.
I'm hardly awake on our morning walk

—always just me and Arden now—
and sometimes I am still
in the thrall of the dream,

which is why, when he took a step onto Commercial
before I'd looked both ways,
I screamed his name and grabbed his collar.

And there I was on my knees,
both arms around his neck
and nothing coming,

and when I looked into that bewildered face
I realized I didn't know what it was
I was shouting at,

I didn't know who I was trying to protect."

2. Reprieve

I woke in the night
and thought, *It was a dream,*

nothing has torn the future apart,
we have not lived years

in dread, it never happened,
I dreamed it all. And then

there was this sensation of terrific pressure
lifting, as if I were rising

in one of those old diving bells,
lightening, unburdening. I didn't know

how heavy my life had become—so much fear,
so little knowledge. It was like

being young again, but I understood
how light I was, how without encumbrance—

and so I felt both young and awake,
which I never felt

when I *was* young. The curtains moved
—it was still summer, all the windows open—

and I thought, I can move that easily.
I thought my dream had lasted for years,

a decade, a dream can seem like that,
I thought, *There's so much more time . . .*

And then of course the truth
came floating back to me.

You know how children
love to end stories they tell

by saying, It was all a dream? Years ago,
when I taught kids to write,

I used to tell them this ending spoiled things,
explaining and dismissing

what had come before. Now I know
how wise they were, to prefer

that gesture of closure,
their stories rounded not with a sleep

but a waking. What other gift
comes close to a reprieve?

This was the dream that Wally told me:
I was in the tunnel, he said,

and there really was a light at the end,
and a great being standing in the light.

His arms were full of people, men and women,
but his proportions were all just right—I mean

he was the size of you or me.
And the people said, Come with us,

we're going dancing. And they seemed so glad
to be going, and so glad to have me

join them, but I said,
I'm not ready yet. I didn't know what to do,

when he finished,
except hold the relentless

weight of him, I didn't know
what to say except, *It was a dream,*

146

nothing's wrong now,
it was only a dream.

3. Michael's Dream

Michael writes to tell me his dream:
I was helping Randy out of bed,
supporting him on one side
with another friend on the other,

and as we stood him up, he stepped out
of the body I was holding and became
a shining body, brilliant light
held in the form I first knew him in.

This is what I imagine will happen,
the spirit's release. Michael,
when we support our friends,
one of us on either side, our arms

under the man or woman's arms,
what is it we're holding? Vessel,
shadow, hurrying light? All those years
I made love to a man without thinking

how little his body had to do with me;
now, diminished, he's never been so plainly
himself—remote and unguarded,
an otherness I can't know

the first thing about. I said,
You need to drink more water
or you're going to turn into
an old dry leaf. And he said,

Maybe I want to be an old leaf.
In the dream Randy's leaping into
the future, and still here; Michael's holding him
and releasing at once. Just as Steve's

holding Jerry, though he's already gone,
Marie holding John, gone, Maggie holding
her John, gone, Carlos and Darren
holding another Michael, gone,

and I'm holding Wally, who's going.
Where isn't the question,
though we think it is;
we don't even know where the living are,

in this raddled and unraveling "here."
What is the body? Rain on a window,
a clear movement over whose gaze?
Husk, leaf, little boat of paper

and wood to mark the speed of the stream?
Randy and Jerry, Michael and Wally
and John: lucky we don't have to know
what something is in order to hold it.

4. Atlantis

I thought your illness a kind of solvent
dissolving the future a little at a time;

I didn't understand what's to come
was always just a glimmer

up ahead, veiled like the marsh
gone under its tidal sheet

148

of mildly rippled aluminum.
What these salt distances were

is also where they're going:
from blankly silvered span

toward specificity: the curve
of certain brave islands of grass,

temporary shoulder-wide rivers
where herons ply their twin trades

of study and desire. I've seen
two white emissaries unfold

like heaven's linen, untouched,
enormous, a fluid exhalation. Early spring,

too cold yet for green, too early
for the tumble and wrack of last season

to be anything but promise,
but there in the air was the triumph

of all flowering, the soul
lifted up, if we could still believe

in the soul, after so much diminishment . . .
Breath, from the unpromising waters,

up, across the pond and the two-lane highway,
pure purpose, over the dune,

gone. Tomorrow's unreadable
as this shining acreage;

the future's nothing
but this moment's gleaming rim.

Now the tide's begun
its clockwork turn, pouring,

in the day's hourglass,
toward the other side of the world,

and our dependable marsh reappears
—emptied of that starched and angular grace

that spirited the ether, lessened,
but here. And our ongoingness,

what there'll be of us? Look,
love, the lost world

rising from the waters again:
our continent, where it always was,

emerging from the half light,
drenched, unchanged.

5. Coastal

Cold April and the neighbor girl
　　—our plumber's daughter—
　　　　comes up the wet street

from the harbor carrying,
　　in a nest she's made
　　　　of her pink parka,

a loon. *It's so sick,*
 she says when I ask.
  Foolish kid,

does she think she can keep
 this emissary of air?
  Is it trust or illness

that allows the head
 —sleek tulip—to bow
  on its bent stem

across her arm?
 Look at the steady,
  quiet eye. She is carrying

the bird back from indifference,
 from the coast
  of whatever rearrangement

the elements intend,
 and the loon allows her.
  She is going to call

the Center for Coastal Studies,
 and will swaddle the bird
  in her petal-bright coat

until they come.
 She cradles the wild form.
  Stubborn girl.

6. New Dog

Jimi and Tony
can't keep Dino,
their cocker spaniel;
Tony's too sick,
the daily walks
more pressure
than pleasure,
one more obligation
that can't be met.

And though we already
have a dog, Wally
wants to adopt,
wants something small
and golden to sleep
next to him and
lick his face.
He's paralyzed now
from the waist down,

whatever's ruining him
moving upward, and
we don't know
how much longer
he'll be able to pet
a dog. How many men
want another attachment,
just as they're
leaving the world?

Wally sits up nights
and says, *I'd like
some lizards, a talking bird,*

some fish. A little rat.
So after I drive
to Jimi and Tony's
in the Village and they
meet me at the door and say,
We can't go through with it,

we can't give up our dog,
I drive to the shelter
—just to look—and there
is Beau: bounding and
practically boundless,
one brass concatenation
of tongue and tail,
unmediated energy,
too big, wild,

perfect. He not only
licks Wally's face
but bathes every
irreplaceable inch
of his head, and though
Wally can no longer
feed himself he can lift
his hand, and bring it
to rest on the rough gilt

flanks when they are,
for a moment, still.
I have never seen a touch
so deliberate.
It isn't about grasping;
the hand itself seems
almost blurred now,
softened, though

tentative only
because so much will
must be summoned,
such attention brought
to the work—which is all
he is now, this gesture
toward the restless splendor,
the unruly, the golden,
the animal, the new.

IN THE COMMUNITY GARDEN

It's almost over now,
late summer's accomplishment,
and I can stand face to face

with this music,
eye to seed-paved eye
with the sunflowers' architecture:

such muscular leaves,
the thick stems' surge.
Though some are still

shiningly confident,
others can barely
hold their heads up;

their great leaves wrap the stalks
like lowered shields. This one
shrugs its shoulders;

this one's in a rush
to be nothing but form.
Even at their zenith,

you could see beneath the gold
the end they'd come to.
So what's the use of elegy?

If their work
is this skyrocket passage
through the world,

is it mine to lament them?
Do you think they'd want
to bloom forever?

It's the trajectory they desire—
believe me, they do
desire, you could say they are

one intent, finally,
to be this leaping
green, this bronze haze

bending down. How could they stand
apart from themselves
and regret their passing,

when they are a field
of lifting and bowing faces,
faces ringed in flames?

TUNNEL MUSIC

Times Square, the shuttle's quick chrome
flies open and the whole car floods with
—what is it? Infernal industry, the tunnels
under Manhattan broken into hell at last?

Guttural churr and whistle and grind
of the engines that spin the poles?
Enormous racket, ungodly. What it is
is percussion: nine black guys

with nine lovely and previously unimagined
constructions of metal ripped and mauled,
welded and oiled: scoured chemical drums,
torched rims, unnamable disks of chrome.

Artifacts of wreck? The end of industry?
A century's failures reworked, bent,
hammered out, struck till their shimmying
tumbles and ricochets from tile walls:

anything dinged, busted or dumped
can be beaten till it sings.
A kind of ghostly joy in it, though
this music's almost unrecognizable,

so utterly of the coming world it is.

CRÊPE DE CHINE

These drugstore windows
—one frame in the mile-long film
of lit-up trash and nothing

fronting the avenue, what Balzac called
"the great poem of display"—
are a tableau of huge bottles

of perfume, unbuyable gallons of scent
for women enormous as the movie screens
of my childhood. Spiritual pharmaceuticals

in their deco bottles,
wide-shouldered, flared,
arrayed in their pastel skylines,

their chrome-topped tiers:
a little Manhattan of tinted alcohols.
Only reading their names

—Mme. Rochas, White Shoulders, Crêpe de Chine—
and I'm hearing the suss of immense stockings,
whispery static of chiffon stoles

on powdered shoulders,
click of compacts, lisp and soft glide
of blush. And I'm thinking of my wig,

my blonde wig, and following the cold sparkle
of pavement I'm wanting not
these shoes but the black clatter

and covenant of heels. Next door
the Italian baker's hung a canopy of garlands
and silver shot, bee lights and silk ivy

high over the sugary excess
of his pastries, and I want
not his product but his display:

I want to wear it,
I want to put the whole big thing
on my head, I want

the tumbling coiffeurs of heaven,
or lacking that, a wig
tiered and stunning as this island.

That's what I want from the city:
to wear it.
That's what drag is: a city

to cover our nakedness,
silk boulevards, sleek avenues
of organza, the budding trees'

along the avenue flaunting their haze
of poisonous Caravaggio green . . .
Look how I take the little florists' shops

and twist them into something
for my hair, forced spiky branches
and a thousand tulips. Look, my sleety veil

of urbane rain descends, unrolls
like cinema's dart and flicker, my skirt
in its ravaged sleekness, the shadows

between buildings raked and angled
into these startling pleats,
descending twilight's gabardine

over the little parks and squares
circled by taxis' hot jewels:
my body

made harmonious with downtown.
Look how I rhyme with the skyscraper's
padded sawtooth shoulders,

look at the secret evidence of my slip
frothing like the derelict river
where the piers used to be,

look at my demolished silhouette,
my gone and reconstructed profile,
look at me built and rebuilt,

torn down to make way,
excavated, trumped up, tricked out,
done, darling,

in every sense of the word. Now,
you call me
Evening in Paris, call me Shalimar,

call me Crêpe de Chine.

HOMO WILL NOT INHERIT

Downtown anywhere and between the roil
of bathhouse steam—up there the linens of joy
and shame must be laundered again and again,

all night—downtown anywhere
and between the column of feathering steam
unknotting itself thirty feet above the avenue's

shimmered azaleas of gasoline,
between the steam and the ruin
of the Cinema Paree (marquee advertising

its own milky vacancy, broken showcases sealed,
ticket booth a hostage wrapped in tape
and black plastic, captive in this zone

of blackfronted bars and bookstores
where there's nothing to read
but longing's repetitive texts,

where desire's unpoliced, or nearly so)
someone's posted a xeroxed headshot
of Jesus: permed, blond, blurred at the edges

as though photographed through a greasy lens,
and inked beside him, in marker strokes:
HOMO WILL NOT INHERIT. *Repent & be saved.*

I'll tell you what I'll inherit: the margins
which have always been mine, downtown after hours
when there's nothing left to buy,

the dreaming shops turned in on themselves,
seamless, intent on the perfection of display,
the bodegas and offices lined up, impenetrable:

edges no one wants, no one's watching. Though
the borders of this shadow-zone (mirror and dream
of the shattered streets around it) are chartered

by the police, and they are required,
some nights, to redefine them. But not now, at twilight,
permission's descending hour, early winter darkness

pillared by smoldering plumes. The public city's
ledgered and locked, but the secret city's boundless;
from which do these tumbling towers arise?

I'll tell you what I'll inherit: steam,
and the blinding symmetry of some towering man,
fifteen minutes of forgetfulness incarnate.

I've seen flame flicker around the edges of the body,
pentecostal, evidence of inhabitation.
And I have been possessed of the god myself,

I have been the temporary apparition
salving another, I have been his visitation, I say it
without arrogance, I have been an angel

for minutes at a time, and I have for hours
believed—without judgment, without condemnation—
that in each body, however obscured or recast,

is the divine body—common, habitable—
the way in a field of sunflowers
you can see every bloom's

the multiple expression
of a single shining idea,
which is the face hammered into joy.

I'll tell you what I'll inherit:
stupidity, erasure, exile
inside the chalked lines of the police,

who must resemble what they punish,
the exile you require of me,
you who's posted this invitation

to a heaven nobody wants.
You who must be patrolled,
who adore constraint, I'll tell you

what I'll inherit, not your pallid temple
but a real palace, the anticipated
and actual memory, the moment flooded

by skin and the knowledge of it,
the gesture and its description
—do I need to say it?—

the flesh *and* the word. And I'll tell you,
you who can't wait to abandon your body,
what you want me to, maybe something

like you've imagined, a dirty story:
Years ago, in the baths,
a man walked into the steam,

the gorgeous deep indigo of him gleaming,
solid tight flanks, the intricately ridged abdomen—
and after he invited me to his room,

nudging his key toward me
as if perhaps I spoke another tongue
and required the plainest of gestures,

after we'd been, you understand,
worshipping a while in his church,
he said to me, *I'm going to punish your mouth.*

I can't tell you what that did to me.
My shame was redeemed then;
I won't need to burn in the afterlife.

It wasn't that he hurt me,
more than that: the spirit's transactions
are enacted now, here—no one needs

your eternity. This failing city's
radiant as any we'll ever know,
paved with oily rainbow, charred gates

jeweled with tags, swoops of letters
over letters, indecipherable as anything
written by desire. I'm not ashamed

to love Babylon's scrawl. How could I be?
It's written on my face as much as on
these walls. This city's inescapable,

gorgeous, and on fire. I have my kingdom.

MIGRATORY

Near evening, in Fairhaven, Massachusetts,
seventeen wild geese arrowed the ashen blue
over the Wal-Mart and the Blockbuster Video,

and I was up there, somewhere between the asphalt
and their clear dominion—not in the parking lot,
its tallowy circles just appearing,

the shopping carts shining, from above,
like little scraps of foil. Their eyes
held me there, the unfailing gaze

of those who know how to fly in formation,
wing tip to wing tip, safe, fearless.
And the convex glamor of their eyes carried

the parking lot, the wet field
troubled with muffler shops
and stoplights, the arc of highway

and its exits, one shattered farmhouse
with its failing barn . . . The wind
a few hundred feet above the grass

erases the mechanical noises, everything;
nothing but their breathing
and the rowing of the pinions,

and then, out of that long, percussive pour
toward what they are most certain of,
comes their—question, is it?

Assertion, prayer, aria—as delivered
by something too compelled in its passage
to sing? A hoarse and unwieldy music

which plays nonetheless down the length
of me until I am involved in their flight,
the unyielding necessity of it, as they literally

rise above, ineluctable, heedless,
needing nothing . . . Only animals
make me believe in God now

—so little between spirit and skin,
any gesture so entirely themselves.
But I wasn't with them,

as they headed toward Acushnet
and New Bedford, of course I wasn't,
though I was not exactly in the parking lot

either, where the cars nudged in and out
of their slots, each taking the place another
had abandoned, so that no space, no desire

would remain unfilled. I wasn't there.
I was so filled with longing
—is that what that sound is for?—

I seemed to be nowhere at all.

NOCTURNE IN BLACK AND GOLD

Shadow is the queen of colors.

—SAINT AUGUSTINE

Tonight the harbor's
    one lustrous wall, the air a warm gray
        —mourning dove, moleskin, gabardine—

blurring the bay's black unguent.
    And, gradually, a few light patches
        —boats? ghosts of lamps

where the pier ends?
    The memory of lamps?
        In Whistler's "Nocturnes"

you can barely see
    the objects of perception,
        or rather there are no solids,

only fitful integers
    of gleam, traces
        of a rocket's shatter,

light troubling a shiver of light.
    Fogged channels, a phantom glow
        on the face of this harbor,

midway between form and void,
    without edges, hypnagogic.
        Listen, I carry myself

like a cigarette lighter
    wrapped between hands in the dark
        and so feel at home in the huge

indefinition of fog, the same
      sort of billowing I am: charcoal, black on black,
            matte on velveteen, a hurrying sheen

on gleaming docks. Keats: *If a Sparrow*
      come before my Window
            I take part in its existence

and pick about the Gravel.
      If we're only volatile essence,
            permeable, leaking out,

pouring into any vessel bright enough
      to lure us, why be afraid?
            Having been a thousand things,

why not be endless?
      Act II, *Die Zauberflöte*:
            the Queen of the Night

ascends her lunar glissando,
      soprano cascading upward
            until you'd swear

this isn't a voice at all;
      she's become an instrument,
            an instant's pure

erasure, essence slipped
      into this florid scatter:
            rhinestones shivering

on a tray lacquered black
      with coldest ozone. *Königin*,
            Königin der Nacht:

chill shine, icy traces . . .
  Here, at wharf's end,
    the trawlers' winking candles

all undone, phantoms
  nearly extinguished
    by the cool salve

of fog. Haven't we wanted,
  all along, to try on boundlessness
    like mutable, starry clothes?

Isn't it a pleasure,
  finally, to be vaporous,
    to be cloudy flares

like these blurred lamps,
  ready to shift or disperse
    or thin to a glaze of atmosphere,

sheer, rarefied, without limit?
  Königin der Nacht: that dizzying pour
    is a voice becoming no one's,

one empty glove
  brushing the evening's cold cheek
    like the clear exhalation

of a star. Against the firmament's
  gleaming patent,
    the Queen's voice

no longer even human:
  a gilt thread raveling
    in the dark. How lucky,

vanishing, to become *that,*
		at once evanescent
			and indelible. Love,

little pilot flame, flickering,
		listen: I've been no one
			so many times I'm not the least afraid.

Doesn't everything rush
		to be something else?
			Won't it be like this,

where you're going: shore and bay,
		harbor and heaven one continuum
			sans coast or margins?

No one's here,
		or hardly anyone, and how strangely
			free and fine it is

to be laved and extended, furthered
		in darkness, while shadows
			give way to other shadows,

and the bay murmurs
		its claim: *You're a rippling,*
			that quick, and you long to be

loose as air again, unfettered
		freshness, atmosphere
			and aria, an aspect of fog,

manifest, and then dissolving,
		which you could regret
			no more than fog.

A brave candling theory
    I'm making for you,
        little lamplight; believe,

and ripple out free
    as shimmer is. Go.
        Don't go. Go.

BEACH ROSES

What are they, the white roses,
when they are almost nothing,
only a little denser than the fog,

shadow-centered petals blurring,
toward the edges, into everything?

This morning one broken cloud
built an archipelago,
                         fourteen gleaming islands

hurrying across a blank plain of sheen:
nothing, or next to nothing

—pure scattering, light on light,
fleeting.
           And now, a heap of roses
beside the sea, white rugosa
beside the foaming hem of shore:
                              brave,

waxen candles . . .

             And we talk
as if death were a line to be crossed.
Look at them, the white roses.
Tell me where they end.

GROSSE FUGE

This October morning,
soft lavender bursts above the Plymouth
parked on the neighbors' lawn: lilacs, wildly
off schedule, decking themselves a second time.
Downtown, on the Universalist green,
the chestnuts drop their sleek mahogany
under lanterned branches, tallowy blooms:
season of contradictions, tempest-wrought.
Summer's hurricane battered each branch bare,
skies suddenly wider, space in heaven
opened, our garden scoured as if by frost.
The little stars' jewel fires more consuming.
That was August, but all at once we wanted
to unpack sweaters, wrap ourselves in warm,
saturated tones: gems and harvest, moss.
But when real autumn came, the calendar
down to its last, late pages, the world
displayed its strange dependability
in disarray, rekindling: crocus
quickened, spiking through the fallen leaves,
then cherry and box elder budded out,
and now this rash, breathtakingly sudden
bloom.
          Bobby arrives on a Saturday,
and sits on the end of the couch, scarlet
parka and a red Jamaican hat fished
from the closet pulled tight. Why's he so cold?
This false spring? No, he looks—how to say it?
—small, not just his circumstances but him
somehow reduced. His landlord doesn't want
him back, his sister's dropped him on the side
of the highway, at a rest stop, his clothes

in three flowered yellow pillowcases.
My mother, he says, doesn't want me
crying in the house; she doesn't want
my tears around. She fed him on paper plates,
kept his laundry separate and didn't tell
his father the diagnosis. We say
of course he can stay and Sunday he wakes
saying, *I have four things inside me:*
a backyard going around and around
in my head this way, lawn furniture
spinning the other way, and right here,

in my chest, chairs. It's not that they hurt,
it's that I can't figure how I'm going
to get them the fuck out. He never says just what
the fourth thing is.
                         This month the new comes
so dizzyingly quick it coexists
with all autumn's evidence: by the marsh,
the usual sumptuous russets, sparked
by pointillist asters. Rugosas dot
the goldenrods' velveteen. Tulips sprout,
the crab leafs out. How are we to read
this nameless season—renewal, promise,
confusion? Should we be glad or terrified
at how quickly things are replaced?
Never again the particulars
of that August garden: waving cosmos,
each form's crisp darkness in relief
against the stars. No way to *know* what's gone,
only the new flowerings, the brilliance
that candles after rain; every day
assuming its position in the huge
gorgeous hurry of budding and decline:

bloom against dry leaf, unreconciled sorts
of evidence.
             I have been teaching myself
to listen to Beethoven, or trying to—
learning to *hear* the late quartets: how hard
it is, to apprehend something so large
in scale and yet so minutely detailed.
Like trying to familiarize yourself,
exactly, with the side of a mountain:
this birch, this rock-pool, this square mosaic
yard of tesserated leaves, autumnal,
a jeweled reliquary. Trying to see
each element of the mountain and then
through them, the whole, since music is only
given to us in time, each phrase parcelled
out, in time.
             Thursday he says *All night*
I had to make Elizabeth Taylor's
wedding cake. It was a huge cake,
with nine towers, all of them spurting
like fountains, and she didn't like it,
and I had to make it again, then
the thing was it wasn't really a cake
anymore.
             I am trying to understand
the *Grosse Fuge*, though I'm not sure what
it might mean to "understand" this stream
of theme and reiteration, statement
and return. What does it mean, chaos
gathered into a sudden bronze sweetness,
an October flourish, and then that moment
denied, turned acid, disassembling,
questioned, rephrased?
                    MRI: charcoaled flowers,
soft smudges, the image that is Bobby,

or Bobby's head, or rather a specific
plane bisecting his head pictured on video,
cinematic, rich inky blacks, threaded
by filaments and clouds. I stand behind
the door, and watch the apparition
taking form beyond the silhouette
of the technician who wore gloves to touch him
(fully clothed, dry, harmless, but the coward
wrapped himself in latex charms anyway,
to ward off the black angel). On the screen,
like a game, he makes a Bobby of light,
numbers, and images—imagines?—Bobby
as atoms of hydrogen, magnetic,
aligned, so that radio waves transmitted
toward the body bounce back, broadcasting
this coal-smudged sketch: brain floating
on its thick stem, and little strokes of dark
everywhere, an image I can't read,
and wasn't supposed to see—but who could
stay away from the door? Which of these
darknesses, if any, is the one which
makes his bed swim at night with boxes,
insistent forms, repeated, rearranged?
In one of those, he says, *is the virus,*
a box of AIDS. And if I open it . . .
I bring home, from each walk to town, pockets
full of chestnuts, and fill a porcelain
bowl with their ruddy, seducing music
—something like cellos, something that banks deep
inside the body. The chestnuts seem lit
from within, almost as if by lamplight,
and burnished to warm leather, the color
of old harnesses . . .

I have four bottles,
cut glass cologne bottles, right here, under
my ribs, by my heart. Can you tell the doctor?
I can't, he doesn't like me.
                              Scribbled notes,
Opus 130: first movement: everything
rises to this sweetness, each previous note
placed now in context, completed, once
the new phrase blooms. Second movement: presto,
skittering summation of the first.
Next, andante broken open
by the force of feeling it contains,
tumbling out into moments of intense
punctuation, like blazing sumac,
goldenrod so densely interwoven
in the field I can't keep any of it
separate for long: pattern of cadence,
spilling out, forward, then cessations.
Like seeing, in jeweled precision,
exact, wet and startlingly *there,* oak leaves,
and birch, and exclamations of maple:
the flecked details of the piebald world.
Seeing it all, taking it in, and yet
rising up to see at once whole forests . . .
Is that it? All my work of listening,
and have I only learned that Beethoven
could see the forest and the trees?
                              Bobby
cries on the couch: *All I want is one head.*
Later, *My head and my legs are one thing.*
Over breakfast: *Please, you've got to tell me,*
the truth now, no matter what, swear.
The boxes, do they ever hold still?
They're driving me crazy with their dancing.
Mostly he looks away, mouth open,

as if studying something slightly above
and to the right of the world.
                            The music
is like lying down in that light which gleams
out of chestnuts, the glow of oiled and rubbed
mahogany, of burled walnut, bird's-eye
maple polished into incandescence:
autumn's essence of brass and resin, bronze
and apples, the evanescent's brisk smoke.
But how is a quartet—abstract thing—
passionate, autumnal, fitful, gleaming,
regretful, hesitant, authoritative,
true? Is any listening an act
of translation, a shift of languages?
Even the music words themselves may make?
Flutter of pendant birch. Then I pull
myself back from the place where the music
has brought me; the music is not leaves,
music is not Bobby's illness; music,
itself, is always *structure*: redolent,
suggestive occasion, a sort of scaffold
which supports the branching of attention.

After the flood of detail the quartet
conjures, nothing: the great block of silence
which the fugue has defined around itself.
When I was seventeen, and everyone
I knew acquired a new vocabulary—*mantra,
sutra, Upanishads*—I learned a chant,
in Sanskrit, *gate gate para gate*
is all I can remember of the words
but the translation goes *gone gone beyond
gone, altogether beyond gone*, and that
is where the music has gone, and Bobby's
going,

though not today, not yet. AZT's
a toxic, limited miracle, and
Bobby's in the kitchen, banging
the teakettle, cursing the oatmeal,
the first time he's been up in weeks. Last night,
when a Supremes song graced the radio,
he suddenly rose, coiffed in his blanket,
and lip-synched twenty seconds of blessed,
familiar drag routine. He's well enough
to be a bitch, to want a haircut
and a shave. Still too sick to go home,
—wherever that might be—and too ill, as well,
to stay: the truth is we can't live
in such radical proximity to his dying.
But not today. In the wet black yard,
October lilacs. Misplaced fever? False flowering,
into the absence the storm supplied?
Flower of the world's beautiful will
to fill, fill space, always to take up space,
hold a place for the possible? A little
flourish, a false spring? What can I do but echo
myself, vary and repeat? Where can the poem end?
What can you expect, in a world that blooms
and freezes all at once?
There is no resolution in the fugue.

from
SWEET MACHINE
(1998)

VISITATION

When I heard he had entered the harbor,
and circled the wharf for days,
I expected the worst: shallow water,

confusion, some accident to bring
the young humpback to grief.
Don't they depend on a compass

lodged in the salt-flooded folds
of the brain, some delicate
musical mechanism to navigate

their true course? How many ways,
in our century's late iron hours,
might we have led him to disaster?

That, in those days, was how
I'd come to see the world:
dark upon dark, any sense

of spirit an embattled flame
sparked against wind-driven rain
till pain snuffed it out. I thought,

This is what experience gives us,
and I moved carefully through my life
while I waited . . . Enough,

it wasn't that way at all. The whale
—exuberant, proud maybe, playful,
like the early music of Beethoven—

cruised the footings for smelts
clustered near the pylons
in mercury flocks. He

(do I have the gender right?)
would negotiate the rusty hulls
of the Portuguese fishing boats

—Holy Infant, Little Marie—
with what could only be read
as pleasure, coming close

then diving, trailing on the surface
big spreading circles
until he'd breach, thrilling us

with the release of pressured breath,
and the bulk of his sleek young head
—a wet black leather sofa

already barnacled with ghostly lice—
and his elegant and unlikely mouth,
and the marvelous afterthought of the flukes,

and the way his broad flippers
resembled a pair of clownish gloves
or puppet hands, looming greenish white

beneath the bay's clouded sheen.
When he had consumed his pleasure
of the swarm, his pleasure, perhaps,

in his own admired performance,
he swam out the harbor mouth,
into the Atlantic. And though grief

has seemed to me itself a dim,
salt suspension in which I've moved,
blind thing, day by day,

through the wreckage, barely aware
of what I stumbled toward, even I
couldn't help but look

at the way this immense figure
graces the dark medium,
and shines so: heaviness

which is no burden to itself.
What did you think, that joy
was some slight thing?

WHERE YOU ARE

1.

flung to your salt parameters   in all that wide gleam
unbounded edgeless   in that brilliant intersection

where we poured   the shattered grit the salt
and distillation of you   which blew back

into my face stinging   like a kiss
from the other world   a whole year

you've languished blue   in ceaseless wind
naked now in all lights   and chill swaddlings

of cloud never for a moment   cold you are
uninterruptible seamless   as if all this time

you'd been sleeping   in the sparkle and beckon
of it are you   in the pour of it

as if there were a secret   shining room
in the house and you'd   merely gone there

we used to swim   summers remember
naked in those shoals   now I think was I ever

that easy   in this life
fireworks remember   Handel an orchestra

on a barge   in the harbor and fountains
spun to darkness   flung in time to

the music scrawling heaven   like sperm like
chrysanthemums bursting   in an enormous hurry

all fire and chatter   flintspark and dazzle
and utterly gone   save here in the scribble

of winter sunlight   on sheer mercury
when I was a child   some green Fourth

flares fretting   the blue-black night
a twirling bit of ash   fell in my open eye

and for a while I couldn't see   those skyrockets
is it like that now love   some cinder

blocking my sight   so that I can't see you
who are only for an hour   asleep and dreaming

in this blue   and light-shot room
as if I could lean across   this shifting watery bed

and ask   are you awake

2.

I thought I'd lost you. But you said *I'm imbued*

in the fabric of things, the way
wax lost from batik shapes
the pattern where the dye won't take.
I make the space around you,

and so allow you shape. And always
you'll feel the traces of that wax
soaked far into the weave:
the air around your gestures,

the silence after you speak.
That's me, that slight wind between
your hand and what you're reaching for;
chair and paper, book or cup:

that close, where I am: between
where breath ends, air starts.

FOG SUITE

1. A Five-Paneled Screen

Fog-lacquered,
varnished in thin
pearl glaze,

the high dunes unfold,
a smudged sketch
for a folding screen,

panels inlaid
with cloudy ivory,
irregular patches

of grassy jade.
(The wide bay's
oddly still this morning,

despite the white activity
at its edges; just beyond the shore's
a huge, silvered equipoise.)

The fog is thinking
of burning away,
but for now

damp scarves
(unhemmed, like petals
of a white peony)

slide and tear
across this portion
of sky, sheets

of smudged paper
hung from heaven.
Trope on trope!

What I'm trying to do
is fix this impossible
shift and flux, and say

how this fog-fired
green's intensified
by sunlight filtered

through the atmosphere's
wet linens—a green
you could almost drink!

No trick of light
I'm talking about
but defiant otherness:

this sky's all
gorgeous trouble,
rain beginning

to fold the screen away.
Do we love more
what we can't say?

As if what we wanted
were to be brought
that much closer

to words' failure,
where desire begins?

2.

What I love about language
is what I love about fog:
what comes between us and things
grants them their shine. Take,

for instance, this estuary,
raised to a higher power
by airy sun-struck voile:
gunmetal cove and glittered bar

hung on the rim of the sky
like palaces in Tibet—
white buildings unreachable,
dreamed and held

at just that perfect distance:
the world's lustered by the veil.

3.

Or else I love fog
because it shows the world

as page, where much
has been written, and much erased.

Clapboards lose their boundaries,
and phantoms of summer's roses

loom like parade floats lost at sea.
Is that what it is,

visible uncertainty?
This evening the thin fact of it

appears a little at a time,
shawling streetlamps,

veiling the heights:
clocktower and steeple gone

in roiling insubstantiality.
I take fog as evidence,

a demonstration of the nothing
(or the nothing much)

that holds the world in place
—rehearsal for our roles

as billow and shroud, drift
and cloud and vanishing act.

And, between these figuring lines,
white space, without which

who could read? Every poem's
half erased. I'm not afraid;

it feels like home here,
held—like any line of text—

by the white margins
of a ghost's embrace.

DOOR TO THE RIVER

—*de Kooning*

He means, I think, there's an out,

built of these fistfuls of yellows.
Means, I think, there's a door,

in this passionate and hard-won
approximation, in this rough push

and lemon smear, this difficulty,

there's—what? In the meadows,
yesterday, great heavy presences

of the trees thinking, rimmed

around the perimeter of the field:
pendulous, weighted, trees

here to be emerald pull
and resistance, suspended

their given hour, the meadow arranging itself

into this huge composition which invites
and resists at once, the world's hung

surface: aren't we always wanting
to push beyond it, as if behind the veil

—old lure and spur, old promise—

lay . . . The bright core
breathing? Why can't you just

love sheer play,
dynamic irresolutions

on the surface of the day?

These trees only seem still,
fixed their hour in the rush

and suction from that gate:
can't you just walk between the yellow

word *field* and the green word *door*
and not demand to penetrate

the primed and stubborn scrim
toward some clarity beyond forms?

Written in a sidewalk's new cement:
Be happy it's really all you have.

Happiness? Our possession
is yellow and green, dialectic

occupying the meadows,

arranging for us this moment
and the next (I'm not afraid

to die, I'm afraid to continue
in this tumult of collisions

and vanishing),
                    the ocher word
meadow, the green word *door*.
                    Listen,

there's a door in these yellow handfuls,
these wild strokes.
                    Haven't you walked

into something like happiness but larger?
Just yesterday, inside the meadow's

goldenrod perimeter,
near evening, in the stubble-grass,

eye level with furled umbels
of wild carrot, chains of burr

and burdock and the clovers' half-dry blooms,

I pressed my stomach against
the warm surface of the field,

sunlight drowsing and slanting
toward us while the dogs and I

lay easy and with no need to be
anywhere. We heard a woman calling,

in a European accent, German maybe, her dog,

her chocolate Lab, who was mousing
with great patience and dedication, and she

with her patience and dedication
was calling *Jackie*, *Jackie* without urgency

because she knew that Jackie would come.

That's when I went through
the door. It was her voice,

the name pronounced softly
over and over above the tender

yellow scent of the grass and the hurry

of intimately related and endlessly
varied yellows, the sunflowers'

golden insistences, little violet
spikings in the eyes of the asters

sparking the whole field into something

like a quivering although entirely still,
and still my two curled companions

not sleeping but like me

alert and perhaps also poised
at an instant when the whole ceaseless

push and tumble arrived at some
balance and there was no lack,

nothing missing, and for the duration
of that sheen

—during which you know
this moment of equipoise

is one more movement of light

and flesh and grass passing through
the corridor, the world's wild maw

of dynamic motion—
Jackie, she said, *Jackie*, yellow word,

and for that astonished instant

hung on the other side, permitted
entrance to the steep

core of things you think
of course this is what death

will be. Fine.

WHITE KIMONO

Sleeves of oyster, smoke and pearl,
linings patterned with chrysanthemum flurries,
rippled fields: the import store's

received a shipment of old robes,
cleaned but neither pressed nor sorted,
and the owner's cut the bindings

so the bales of crumpled silks
swell and breathe. It's raining out, off-season,
nearly everything closed,

so Lynda and I spend an hour
overcome by wrinkly luxuries we'd never wear,
even if we could: clouds of—

are they plum blossoms?—
billowing on mauve, thunderheads
of pine mounting a stony slope,

tousled fields of embroidery
in twenty shades of jade:
costumes for some Japanese

midsummer's eve. And there,
against the back wall, a garment
which seems itself an artifact

of dream: tiny gossamer sleeves
like moth wings worrying a midnight lamp,
translucent silk so delicate

it might shatter at the weight
of a breath or glance.
The mere idea of a robe,

a slip of a thing
(even a small shoulder
might rip it apart)

which seems to tremble a little,
in the humid air. The owner—
enjoying our pleasure, this slow afternoon,

in the lush tumble of his wares—
gives us a deal. A struggle, to narrow it
to three: deep blue for Lynda,

lined with a secretive orange splendor
of flowers, a long scholarly gray for me,
severe, slightly pearly, meditative,

a rough raw silk for Wally,
its slubbed green the color of day-old grass
wet against lawn-mower blades. Home,

we iron till the kitchen steams,
revealing drape and luster.
Wally comes out and sits with us, too,

though he's already tired all the time,
and the three of us fog up the rainy windows,
talking, ironing, imagining mulberry acres

spun to this unlikely filament
—nearly animate stuff—and the endless
labor of unwinding the cocoons.

What strength and subtlety in these hues.
Doesn't rain make a memory more intimate?
We're pleased with our own calm privacy,

our part in the work of restoration,
that kitchen's achieved, common warmth,
the time-out-of-time sheen

of happiness to it, unmistakable
as the surface of those silks. And
all the while that fluttering spirit

of a kimono hung in the shop
like a lunar token, something
the ghost of a moth might have worn,

stirring on its hanger whenever
the door was opened—petal, phantom,
little milky flame lifting

like a curtain in the wind
—which even Lynda, slight as she was,
did not dare to try on.

THE EMBRACE

You weren't well or really ill yet either;
just a little tired, your handsomeness
tinged by grief or anticipation, which brought
to your face a thoughtful, deepening grace.

I didn't for a moment doubt you were dead.
I knew that to be true still, even in the dream.
You'd been out—at work maybe?—
having a good day, almost energetic.

We seemed to be moving from some old house
where we'd lived, boxes everywhere, things
in disarray: that was the story of my dream,
but even asleep I was shocked out of narrative

by your face, the physical fact of your face:
inches from mine, smooth-shaven, loving, alert.
Why so difficult, remembering the actual look
of you? Without a photograph, without strain?

So when I saw your unguarded, reliable face,
your unmistakable gaze opening all the warmth
and clarity of you—warm brown tea—we held
each other for the time the dream allowed.

Bless you. You came back, so I could see you
once more, plainly, so I could rest against you
without thinking this happiness lessened anything,
without thinking you were alive again.

MESSIAH (CHRISTMAS PORTIONS)

A little heat caught
in gleaming rags,
in shrouds of veil,
   torn and sun-shot swaddlings:

   over the Methodist roof,
two clouds propose a Zion
of their own, blazing
   (colors of tarnish on copper)

   against the steely close
of a coastal afternoon, December,
while under the steeple
   the Choral Society

   prepares to perform
Messiah, pouring, in their best
blacks and whites, onto the raked stage.
   Not steep, really,

   but from here,
the first pew, they're a looming
cloudbank of familiar angels:
   that neighbor who

   fights operatically
with her girlfriend, for one,
and the friendly bearded clerk
   from the post office

—tenor trapped
in the body of a baritone? Altos
from the A&P, soprano
    from the T-shirt shop:

    today they're all poise,
costume and purpose
conveying the right note
    of distance and formality.

    Silence in the hall,
anticipatory, as if we're all
about to open a gift we're not sure
    we'll like;

    how could they
compete with sunset's burnished
oratorio? Thoughts which vanish,
    when the violins begin.

    Who'd have thought
they'd be so good? *Every valley*,
proclaims the solo tenor,
    (a sleek blond

    I've seen somewhere before
—the liquor store?) *shall be exalted*,
and in his handsome mouth the word
    is lifted and opened

    into more syllables
than we could count, central *ah*
dilated in a baroque melisma,
    liquefied; the pour

of voice seems
to *make* the unplaned landscape
the text predicts the Lord
    will heighten and tame.

    This music
demonstrates what it claims:
glory shall be revealed. If art's
    acceptable evidence,

    mustn't what lies
behind the world be at least
as beautiful as the human voice?
    The tenors lack confidence,

    and the soloists,
half of them anyway, don't
have the strength to found
    the mighty kingdoms

    these passages propose
—but the chorus, all together,
equals my burning clouds,
    and seems itself to burn,

    commingled powers
deeded to a larger, centering claim.
These aren't anyone we know;
    choiring dissolves

    familiarity in an up-
pouring rush which will not
rest, will not, for a moment,
    be still.

Aren't we enlarged
by the scale of what we're able
to desire? Everything,
    the choir insists,

    might flame;
inside these wrappings
burns another, brighter life,
    quickened, now,

    by song: hear how
it cascades, in overlapping,
lapidary waves of praise? Still time.
    Still time to change.

SHELTER

They shove
    and tumble around us
        on the concrete floor,

the little ones,
    just as they must have crowded
        around the gates of this world,

eager to live. So much
    to be licked, on earth,
        what work! All mouth, sure

of their reception,
    they've hurried to a realm
        they know will feed them,

so they open their new faces
    to us, tongues and teeth
        apprehending our scents

and salts. *This is here*,
    the minds register, *yes*,
        and this, and this is good.

The older ones, each
    in a separate pen, consider
        what's to be made

of betrayal. This one's
    all evident eagerness,
        muzzle against the grid;

this one serenely still,
    waiting for us to make
        the first gesture, though

there's something—hopeful?—
    in his expression. The one
        who's been here longest

cries, though not to us.
    Rowed under
        the hellgate inscriptions

(*Too big, No time,*
    Landlord says no)
        they've lost habitations

and, some of them, names,
    though most carry forward
        a single word—

Tahoe, Dakota, Jack—
    all of the past they're allowed
        to keep, and not enough

to stop the world from draining
    into this vague limbo
        far from affection's locations

and routines. I know.
    Leashed to no one,
        the plain daily habits

gone, who are we?
    No one's dog
        is nothing but eagerness

tempered with caution,
    though only a little.
        We wanted to be born

once, don't we want
    to be delivered again,
        even knowing the nothing

love may come to?
    O Lucky and Buddy and Red,
        we put our tongues to the world.

LILIES IN NEW YORK

A drawing: smudged shadow, deep worked areas of graphite
rendering exactly a paper-wrapped pot's particular folds, then
each spiculate leaf, their complex spiraling movement up the
stem, and the shining black nodes—seeds?—mounted at the
intersection of stalk and leaf: a work of attention all the way
up to the merest suggestion of the three flowers, a few rough
unmodulated lines . . .

what's this about? Why,

up here where trumpeting
crowns all this darkness,
has the artist given up?

Exhaustion, since he's made such
a density of strokes below?
This page moves from deep,

pressured rendering
toward these slight gestures,
the flower merely sketched,

barely represented. Is it that
he wants us to think, *This is a drawing,
not a flower* and so reminds us

that the power of his illusion,
alive below the lily's neck,
is trickery? A formal joke,

airy fragility over such a field of marks,
warring masses, particulate suspensions
(lead, black chalk, charred—coal?

smoothed or scribbled or crosshatched everywhere,
a made night): art's dialectic, the done
and undone, dirty worked spaces

and the clean blank gaze of the unfinished,
with all its airy invitations? Or is it
too much for him, to render that delicacy,

to bring the white throat out
of white paper, no hope of accuracy,
and so he makes this humble gesture

to acknowledge his own limitations,
because the lilies are perfect,
is that it, and what version

of their splendor would come any closer
than this wavering, errant line?
Or is he indifferent to flowering,

to culmination and resolution?
Would he rather remain with the push
of areas of darkness, hustle

and dash of line, cacophony of pot
and stem, roiling swoops and scrawls
like clashing swathes of twilight,

furious? As if the frame
were filled with colliding expanses
of noise (traffic, sirens, some engine

hammering into the street below,
barking, air brakes expelling their huge
mechanical tribute to longing,

arc of a train's passage and descent
below the river), as if charcoal
were a medium of solidified sound,

is that it, which allowed the grind
and pull of this city to render itself,
to pour through his hand

into its own representation
—which does not hobble our apprehension
of the thing but honors it, since it is

of the moment only, a singular
clarity, and we understand, don't we,
that stasis is always a lie?

These only appear to be lilies,
this conflation of smudges,
but isn't the ruse lovely,

matter got up in costume as itself?
Isn't the dark carved now,
a moment, around the body

of the flower? New York's
a clutch in which these lilies
are held, let's say the drawing's

subject is Manhattan's grip,
the instant in which the city
constellates itself

around this vertical stroke
risen from a blur of florist's paper:
doesn't all of New York lean

into the hard black lines defining
stalk and leaf, a field of pressure
and distortion, a storm

billowing and forming itself
now around these shapes?
Isn't the city flower and collision?

Trumpet, trumpet, and trumpet:
now New York's a smear
and chaos of lilies, a seized whir,

burr and diminishment, a greased dark
clank of lilies which contains in itself
snowy throat and black crosshatched

field of atmosphere, scent
and explosion, tenderness
and history, all that's leaning

down into the delicate, nearly human skin,
pressing with its impossible weight,
despite which the mouth of the flower

—quick and temporary as
any gesture made by desire—
remains open. Lustrous,

blackening, open as if
about to speak. Open—
is that it? Out of these negotiations

arises a sketchy, possible
bloom, about to, going to,
going to be, becoming

open. And who could hope to draw that?

MY TATTOO

I thought I wanted to wear
the Sacred Heart, to represent
education through suffering,

how we're pierced to flame.
But when I cruised
the inkshop's dragons,

cobalt tigers and eagles
in billowy smokes,
my allegiance wavered.

Butch lexicon,
anchors and arrows,
a sailor's iconic charms—

tempting, but none
of them me. What noun
would you want

spoken on your skin
your whole life through?
I tried to picture what

I'd never want erased
and saw a fire-ring corona
of spiked rays,

flaring tongues
surrounding—an emptiness,
an open space?

I made my mind up.
I sat in the waiting room chair.
Then something (my nerve?

faith in the guy
with biker boots
and indigo hands?)

wavered. It wasn't fear;
nothing hurts like grief,
and I'm used to that.

His dreaming needle
was beside the point;
don't I already bear

the etched and flaring marks
of an inky trade?
What once was skin

has turned to something
made; written and revised
beneath these sleeves:

hearts and banners,
daggers and flowers and names.
I fled. Then I came back again;

isn't there always
a little more room
on the skin? It's too late

to be unwritten,
and I'm much too scrawled
to ever be erased.

Go ahead: prick and stipple
and ink me in:
I'll never be naked again.

From here on out,
I wear the sun,
albeit blue.

METRO NORTH

Over the terminal,
    the arms and chest
        of the god

brightened by snow.
    Formerly mercury,
        formerly silver,

surface yellowed
    by atmospheric sulphurs
        acid exhalations,

and now the shining
    thing's descendant.
        Obscure passages,

dim apertures:
    these clouded windows
        show a few faces

or some empty car's
    filmstrip of lit flames
        —remember them

from school,
    how they were supposed
        to teach us something?—

waxy light hurrying
    inches away from the phantom
        smudge of us, vague

in spattered glass. Then
        daylight's soft charcoal
                lusters stone walls

and we ascend to what
        passes for brightness,
                this February,

scumbled sky
        above graduated zones
                of decline:

dead rowhouses,
        charred windows'
                wet frames

around empty space,
        a few chipboard polemics
                nailed over the gaps,

speeches too long
        and obsessive for anyone
                on this train to read,

sealing the hollowed interiors
        —some of them grand once,
                you can tell by

the fillips of decoration,
        stone leaves, the frieze
                of sunflowers.

Desolate fields—open spaces,
        in a city where you
                can hardly turn around!—

seem to center
      on little flames,
            something always burning

in a barrel or can.
      As if to represent
            inextinguishable,

dogged persistence?
      Though whether what burns
            is will or rage or

harsh amalgam
      I couldn't say.
            But I can tell you this,

what I've seen that
      won my allegiance most,
            though it was also

the hallmark of our ruin,
      and quick as anything
            seen in transit:

where Manhattan ends
      in the narrowing
            geographical equivalent

of a sigh (asphalt,
      arc of trestle, dull-witted
            industrial tanks

and scaffoldings, ancient now,
      visited by no one)
            on the concrete

embankment just
    above the river,
        a sudden density

and concentration
    of trash, so much
        I couldn't pick out

any one thing
    from our rising track
        as it arced onto the bridge

over the fantastic
    accumulation of jetsam
        and contraband

strewn under
    the uncompromising
        vault of heaven.

An unbelievable mess,
    so heaped and scattered
        it seemed the core

of chaos itself—
    but no, the junk was arranged
        in rough aisles,

someone's intimate
    clutter and collection,
        no walls but still

a kind of apartment
    and a fire ribboned out
        of a ruined stove,

and white plates
     were laid out
          on the table beside it.

White china! Something
     was moving, and
          —you understand

it takes longer to tell this
     than to see it, only
          a train window's worth

of actuality—
     I knew what moved
          was an arm,

the arm of the (man
     or woman?) in the center
          of that hapless welter

in layer upon layer
     of coats blankets scarves
          until the form

constituted one more
     gray unreadable;
          whoever

was lifting a hammer,
     and bringing it down
          again, tapping at

what work
     I couldn't say;
          whoever, under

the exhausted dome
of winter light,
which the steep

and steel surfaces of the city
made both more soft
and more severe,

was making something,
or repairing,
was in the act

(sheer stubborn nerve of it)
of putting together.
Who knows what.

(And there was more,
more I'd take all spring
to see. I'd pick my seat

and set my paper down
to study him again
—he, yes, some days not

at home though usually
in, huddled
by the smoldering,

and when my eye wandered
—five-second increments
of apprehension—I saw

he had a dog!
Who lay half in
half out his doghouse

in the rain, golden head
    resting on splayed paws.
        He had a ruined car,

    and heaps of clothes,
    and things to read—
        was no emblem,

in other words,
    but a citizen,
        who'd built a citizen's

household, even
    on the literal edge,
        while I watched

from my quick,
    high place, hurtling
        over his encampment

by the waters of Babylon.)
    Then we were gone,
        in the heat and draft

of our silver, rattling
    over the river
        into the South Bronx,

against whose greasy
    skyline rose that neoned
        billboard for cigarettes

which hostages
    my attention, always,
        as it is meant to do,

its motto ruby
in the dark morning:
ALIVE WITH PLEASURE.

GOLDEN RETRIEVALS

Fetch? Balls and sticks capture my attention
seconds at a time. Catch? I don't think so.
Bunny, tumbling leaf, a squirrel who's—oh
joy—actually scared. Sniff the wind, then

I'm off again: muck, pond, ditch, residue
of any thrillingly dead thing. And you?
Either you're sunk in the past, half our walk,
thinking of what you never can bring back,

or else you're off in some fog concerning
—tomorrow, is that what you call it? My work:
to unsnare time's warp (and woof!), retrieving,
my haze-headed friend, you. This shining bark

a Zen master's bronzy gong, calls you here,
entirely, now: bow-wow, bow-wow, bow-wow.

LILACS IN NYC

Monday evening, E. 22nd
    in front of Jimmy and Vincent's,
a leafing maple, and it's as if

Manhattan existed in order
    to point to these
leaves, the urbane marvel

of them. Tuesday AM
    at the Korean market,
cut, bundled lilacs, in clear

or silvered cellophane—
    mist & inebriation,
cyclonic flames in tubs

of galvanized aluminum,
    all along Third Avenue,
as if from the hardy rootstocks

of these shops sprouted
    every leaf-shine and shade
of panicle: smoke, plum, lavender

like the sky over the Hudson,
    some spring evenings, held
in that intoxicating window

the horizontal streets provide.
    Numbered avenues,
dumb, beautiful ministers . . . Later,

a whole row of white crab apples
   shivering in the wind
of a passing train; later,

a magnolia flaring
   in a scatter
of its own fallen petals,

towering out of a field
   of itself. Is that what
we do? I've felt like that,

straddling my lover,
   as if I rose
out of something

which resembled me,
   joined at the trunk
as if I come flaming

up out of what I am,
   the live foam muscling
beneath me . . .

Strong bole thrust up
   into the billow,
into the frills and the insistences

and elaborations,
   the self flying open!
They're flowers, they know

to fall if they bloom;
   blessed relief of it,
not just myself this little while.

You enter me and we are strangers
   to ourselves but not
to each other, I enter you

(strange verb but what else
   to call it—to penetrate
to fuck to be inside of

none of the accounts of the body
   were ever really useful were they
tell the truth none of them),

I enter you (strange verb,
   as if we were each an enclosure
a shelter, imagine actually

considering yourself a *temple*)
   and violet the crush of shadows
that warm wrist that deep-hollowed

collar socket those salt-lustered
   lilacy shoulder blades
in all odd shadings of green and dusk . . .

blooming in the field
   of our shatter. You enter me
and it's Macy's,

some available version of infinity;
   I enter you and I'm the grass,
covered with your shock

of petals out of which you rise
   Mr. April Mr. Splendor
climbing up with me

inside this rocking, lilac boat.
    My candlelight master,
who trembles me into smoke-violet,

as April does to lilac-wood.

MERCY ON BROADWAY

Saturday, Eighth and Broadway,
a dozen turtles the color of crushed mint

try for the ruby rim
of a white enamel bowl

on the sidewalk, wet jade
jewel cases climbing two

or three times the length
of their bodies toward heaven

till the slick sides of the bowl
send them sliding back into

their brothers' bright heap
of grassy armament. The avenue's

a high wall of what the clubs call
deep house mix: tribal rave

from the flea market across the street,
some deejay hawking forty-five-minute sides

of pure adrenaline, snarl and sputter
and staccato bass of traffic and some idling taxi,

siren wail's high arc over it all,
blocks away, and the call and response

of kids on both sides of the avenue,
some flashing ripple of Motown sparking

the whole exhaust-shimmered tapestry
like gold thread *don't forget*

the motor city and even some devotees'
hare rama droned in for good measure

in the sheer seamless scrim
of sound this town is, so at first

I can't make out the woman
beside me saying *You want buy turtle?*

I don't want any one of this
boiling bowl of coppery citizens

longing for release—a dozen maybe,
or nothing at all. So much to want

in this city, the world's bounty
laid out, what's the point in owning

any one piece of it? Deep house mix:
these hip-hop kids disappearing

into huge jackets and phat jeans,
these Latin girls with altarpiece earrings,

homo boys eyeing each other's big
visible auras of self-consciousness

all the way across Broadway,
vendors from Senegal Hong Kong

and Staten Island selling
incense sweatshirts peanuts

roasted in some burning sugar syrup.
What do you want right now?

What can't the city teach you
to want? It's body atop body here,

lovely and fragile armor dressed up
as tough, it's so many beats there's

something you can dance to, plan on it,
flash and hustle all up and down

this avenue. Don't let it fool you,
grief's going down all over

these blocks, invisible only
because indifferent and ravenous

Broadway swallows it all,
a blowsy appetite just as eager

to eat you as to let you go;
maybe you're someone in particular

but no offense pal no one's necessary
to the big sound of the avenue's

tribal, acid mix.
I'm standing here bent

over this bowl of turtles—
green as Asia, sharp-edged

as lemongrass—and ruthless
as I know this street is

nowhere, nowhere to run to,
nowhere to hide this morning there's no place

I'd rather be than smack in the thrall
of Broadway's merciless matter

and flash, pulse and trouble. *Turtle?*
You want? Their future can't be bright;

what's one live emerald clutch purse
in the confusion and glory

Manhattan is? Listen, I've seen fever
all over this town, no mercy, I've seen

the bodies I most adored turned to flame
and powder, my shattered darlings

a clutch of white petals lifted
on the avenue's hot wind:

last night's lottery tickets
crumpled chances blown in grates

and gutters. I'm forty-one years old
and ready to get down

on my knees to a kitchen bowl
full of live green. I'm breathing here,

a new man next to me who's beginning
to matter. *It's gonna take a miracle*

sings any one of the untraceable radios
or tape decks or personal hookups to the music

of the spheres threading this fluid
and enormous crowd *to make me love*

someone new. I don't think these turtles
are going to make it, but what

does that mean? Maybe an hour
on Broadway's jewel enough.

Unthinkably green now, they're inseparable
from the sudden constellation

of detail the avenue's become
—this boulevard continuously radiant,

if only we could see it—live integers
of this streaming town's

lush life. As you and I are, boy,
laughing and strolling and taking our parts

in its plain vulgar gorgeousness,
its cheap and shining aspirations.

I want what everybody wants,
that's how I know I'm still

breathing: deep mix, rapture
and longing. Let me take your arm,

in that shiny blue jacket I love,
clear plastic pendants hung

like bijoux from its many zippers,
let me stand close to you in the way

the avenue allows, let the sun flash
on your chrome ring, let me praise

your sideburns and your black baseball cap,
signifying gestures that prove

gonna take a miracle we're living.
I've been lucky; I've got a man

in my head who's spirit and ash
and flecks of bone now, and a live one

whose skin is inches from mine.
I've been granted this reprieve,

and I'll take whatever part
Broadway assigns me: Man on His Knees

Beside a Bowl of Turtles, Man on the Sidewalk
with His Heart in His Mouth? Let's walk,

let's drink this city street's
ash and attitude, its human waves

of style and talk, its hundred
thousand ways to say *Hey.*

I looked into that shiny cup
of ambulant green and I thought

Somebody's going to live through this.
Suppose it's you? Whatever happens to me,

to us, somebody's going to ride out
these blasted years, somebody if I'm still lucky

years from now will read this poem and walk
on Broadway. Broadway's no one,

and Broadway lasts. Here's the new
hat, the silhouette of the summer. Here's

the new jewelry everybody's wearing,
the right haircut, the new dance, the new song,

the next step, the new way of walking, the world
that's on everyone's lips, the word that's on its way:

our miracle Broadway, our hour.

from
SOURCE
(2001)

BRIAN AGE SEVEN

Grateful for their tour
of the pharmacy,
the first-grade class
has drawn these pictures,
each self-portrait taped
to the window-glass,
faces wide to the street,
round and available,
with parallel lines for hair.

I like this one best: Brian,
whose attenuated name
fills a quarter of the frame,
stretched beside impossible
legs descending from the ball
of his torso, two long arms
springing from that same
central sphere. He breathes here,

on his page. It isn't craft
that makes this figure come alive;
Brian draws just balls and lines,
in wobbly crayon strokes.
Why do some marks
seem to thrill with life,
possess a portion
of the nervous energy
in their maker's hand?

That big curve of a smile
reaches nearly to the rim
of his face; he holds
a towering ice cream,
brown spheres teetering
on their cone,
a soda fountain gift
half the length of him
—as if it were the flag

of his own country held high
by the unadorned black line
of his arm. Such naked support
for so much delight! Artless boy,
he's found a system of beauty:
he shows us pleasure
and what pleasure resists.
The ice cream is delicious.
He's frail beside his relentless standard.

PAUL'S TATTOO

The flesh dreams toward permanence,

and so this red carp noses from the inked dusk
of a young man's forearm as he tilts

the droning burin of his trade toward
the blank page of my dear one's biceps

—a scene framed, from where I watch,
in an arched mirror, a niche of mercuried glass

the shape of those prosceniums in which still lifes
reside, in cool museum rooms: tulips and medlars,

oysters and snails and flies on permanently
perishing fruit: vanitas. All *is* vanitas,

for these two arms—one figured, one just beginning
to be traced with the outline of a heart—

are surrounded by a cabinet of curiosities,
the tattooist's reflected shelves of skulls

—horses, pigs?—and photos of lobes and nipples
shocked into style. Trappings of evil

unlikely to convince: the shop's called 666,
a casket and a pit bull occupy the vestibule,

but the coffin's pink and the hellhound licked
our faces clean as the latex this bearded boy donned

to prick the veil my lover's skin presents
—rent, now, with a slightly comic heart,

warmly ironic, lightly shaded, and crowned,
as if to mean feeling's queen or king of any day,

certainly this one, a quarter hour
suddenly galvanized by a rippling electric trace

firing adrenaline and an odd sense of limit
defied. Not overcome, exactly; this artist's

filled his shop with evidence of that.
To what else do these clean,

Dutch-white bones testify?
But resistant, still, skin grown less subject

to change, ruled by what is drawn there:
a freshly shadowed *corazón*

now heron-dark, and ringed
by blue exultant bits of sweat or flame—

as if the self contained too much
to be held, and flung out droplets

from the dear proud flesh
—stingingly warm—a steadier hand

has raised into art, or a wound,
or both. The work's done,

our design complete. A bandage,
to absorb whatever pigment

the newly writ might weep,
a hundred guilders, a handshake, back out

onto the street. Now all his life
he wears his heart beneath his sleeve.

TO THE ENGRAVER OF MY SKIN

I understand the pact is mortal,
agree to bear this permanence,

I contract with limitation, I say
no and no then yes to you, and sign

—here, on the dotted line—
for whatever comes, I do: our time,

our outline, the filling-in of our details
(it's density that hurts, always,

not the original scheme). I'm here
for revision, discoloration, here to fade

and last, ineradicable, blue. Write me!
This ink lasts longer than I do.

AT THE GYM

This salt-stain spot
marks the place where men
lay down their heads,
back to the bench,

and hoist nothing
that need be lifted
but some burden they've chosen
this time: more reps,

more weight, the upward shove
of it leaving, collectively,
this sign of where we've been:
shroud-stain, negative

flashed onto the vinyl
where we push something
unyielding skyward,
gaining some power

at least over flesh,
which goads with desire,
and terrifies with frailty.
Who could say who's

added his heat to the nimbus
of our intent, here where
we make ourselves:
something difficult

lifted, pressed or curled,
Power over beauty,
power over power!
Though there's something more

tender, beneath our vanity,
our will to become objects
of desire: we sweat the mark
of our presence onto the cloth.

Here is some halo
the living made together.

LOST IN THE STARS

The Café Musicale,
a benefit organized by Billy—
sweet, irksome Billy,
who seemed fundamentally
incapable of organizing anything,
though he'd managed

to fill a hall, a midwinter Saturday,
the town muffled by snow,
and dozens ready to perform:
girl singers with severely sculptural hair,
earnest poets, West End Wendy,
who played cowgirl tunes

on her ukelele, and a pianist
who'd driven all the way from a lounge
where he was appearing in Hyannis.
Where did Billy find us all?
The cause: PWAs, a fund
for art supplies, paint and clay

and darkroom chemicals.
We filled the folding chairs;
act after act the snow piled up
outside, scrolling the windows
with an intimate, tumbling rhythm,
ethereal. Marie read poems,

and Michael—in a thrift-store retro
ensemble that meant *I want a boyfriend*—
made his literary debut.
Someone played the spoons.
Davíd, who'd said our town
averaged that year a funeral a week,

did a performance piece
about the unreliability of language.
Someone showed slides: family snapshots
tinted the colors of a bruise. (Art heals,
we thought. It was 1992,
and we were powerless.)

We were studiedly casual
in our clothes, which is why
the drag queen who appeared
at intermission startled so:
black glittery leotard, eyelashes
spiking from kohl-rimmed, huge

black eyes, bouffant hard
and black, high thick heels:
it was a wonder she'd come out of the snow.
When she took the stage,
the houselights—though
there were none—dimmed.

The music was Kurt Weill,
"Lost in the Stars." Nothing
overtly funny about it:
since she *was* irony
she did nothing ironic,
only a raised eyebrow,

a subtle turn of the wrist
to acknowledge the ways
the limits of flesh
resisted her ambitions.
A long time, in those lyrics,
before "I" appears,

to tell us the chanteuse
has wandered her way
toward disenchantment:
I've been walking through
the night and the day,
she sang, *and sometimes*

it seems maybe God's
gone away, not without
a certain warmth in those tones,
not without wisdom.
(He is unpossessed
of any special understanding,

daytimes, off work, but she
was a contained storm,
her body's darkness opening,
as if one of the windows
had fallen open, startling us
with that continuous scrolling freefall.)

Then those who'd left someone
home in bed, someone not well enough
to come, began to tug on scarves
and coats. And the half-dozen
who'd been helped to their metal chairs,
canes leaning against them,

men with portals in their necks
or chests for foscarnet
and ganciclovir, who'd clapped
or nodded off while
we raised money for art supplies—
they all went home too.

I walked into the snow
(*I've been walking through
the night and the day*);
Wally was home in bed, blocks away—
sleeping, I hoped, though I'd left him
alone as long as I dared.

I can hardly remember how
it felt now, that relentless
hopelessness. The Musicale,
in the way of such things,
went on long after it was over,
and the next year there was another,

though Billy'd begun to unravel
then, his introductions less sensible,
his imitations of his friends opaque.
No one had the heart
to tell him to sit down.
We'd stay through it;

we'd stay for Billy,
and to buy the men we knew
clay and brushes and sketching paper.
How will I remember them?
I wouldn't have guessed
it would be this: how

—dark and glittering and
strangely self-contained—
she reached her gloved hand
toward us (*We're lost*)
in a gesture unmistakably twofold:
she wanted to touch us,

and we were already,
in her lyric, contained.
This is what imagination
must do, isn't it, find a form?
She dazzled our estrangement.
She asserted her night.

She was the no one we needed;
she sang the necessary,
gleaming emptiness.
You who were taken,
you who are gone now
in the drift and ash of the lyric

we've made of you,
gone into the snowfall
still unreeling somewhere,
repetitive, poised, so relentless
you might take it for stillness,
how will we remember you?

The black glove opens
and there it is, still falling,
beyond memory, beyond recovery,
the snow of 1992.

I have a saucepan of Billy's still; he made a stew for me when Wally died. He spent a whole afternoon seasoning it: parsley, rosemary, oregano. And Peter, at Billy's memorial, was so true to the memory of his friend he seemed almost too exasperated to cry, as if among the thousand irritating things Billy would do, now he'd gone and died. And the best way to keep something of Billy was to hold on to how much he'd annoyed us: in that way we could remember who he was.

MANHATTAN: LUMINISM

The sign said *Immunology*
but I read
Illuminology: and look,

heaven *is* a platinum latitude
over Fifth, fogged result
of sun on brushed

steel, pearl
dimensions. Cézanne:
"We are an iridescent chaos."

 ◆　◆　◆

Balcony over Lexington, May evening,

fog-wreath'd towers,
Gothic dome lit from within,
monument of our aspirations

turned hollow, abandoned

somehow. And later, in the florist's window
on Second, a queen's display
of orchid and fern, lush heap

of dried sheaves, bounty of grasses . . .

What's that? Mice
far from any field
but feasting.

• • •

The sign said
K YS MADE,
but what will op n,

if the locksmith's
lost his vowel
—his entrance,

edge, his means
of egress—
which held together

the four letters
of his trade?
City of consonants,

city of locks,
and he's lost
the E.

• • •

(A Mirror in the Chelsea Hotel)

Here, where odd old things have come to rest
—a lamp that never meant
to keep on going, a chest
whose tropical veneers
are battered and submissive—

this glass gives the old hotel room
back to itself in a warmer atmosphere,
as if its silver were thickening,
a gathering opacity held here,
just barely giving back . . .

This mirror resists what it can,
too weary for generosity.
As if each coming and going,
each visitor turned, one night
or weeks, to check a collar

or the angle of a hat, left some residue,
a bit of leave-taking preserved in mercury.
And now, filled up with all that regard,
there is hardly any room for regarding,
and a silvered fog fills nearly all

the space, like rain: the city's lovely,
crowded dream, which closes you
into itself like a folding screen.

    ♦ ♦ ♦

Almost nightfall, West 82nd,
and a child falls to her knees
on the cement, and presses

herself against the glass
of the video store,
because she wants to hold her face

against the approaching face,
huge, open, on the poster
hung low in the window,

down near the sidewalk:
an elephant walking toward
the viewer, ears wide to the world.

She cries out in delight,
at first, and her mother
acknowledges her pleasure,

but then she's still there,
kneeling, in silence, and no matter
what the mother does or says

the girl's not moving,
won't budge, though her name's
called again and again.

Could you even name it,
what suddenly seems
to rule these streets?

—as if the underlying principle
of the city had been drawn up
from beneath the pavement

by a girl who doesn't know
any better than to insist
on the force of her wish

to look into the gaze which seems
to go on steadily coming toward her,
though of course it isn't moving at all.

◆　◆　◆

I woke in the old hotel.
The shutters were open
in the high, single window;
the light gone delicate, platinum.
What had I been dreaming,

what would become of me now?
There were doves calling,
their three-note tremolo
climbing the airshaft
—something about the depth

of that sound, where it reaches in you,
what it touches. You've been abraded,
something exchanged or given away
with every encounter, on the street,
the train, something of you lost

to the bodies that unnerved you,
in the station, streaming ahead,
everyone going somewhere certain
in the randomly intersecting flow
of our hurry, until you could be anyone,

in the furious commingling . . .
But now you're more awake, aren't you,
and of course these aren't doves,
not in the middle of Manhattan;
a little harsher, more driven,

these pigeons, though recognizable
still in the pulse of their throats
the threnody of their kind, rising
to you or to that interior ear
with which you are always listening,

in the great city, where things are said
to no one, and everyone, and still
it's the same . . . You were afraid
you were edgeless, one bit
of light's indifferent streaming,

and you are—but in a way you also
are singled out, are, in the old sense,
a soul, because you have heard
the thrilling, deep-entering rumple
and susurrus of the birds, and now

a little cadence of sun in motion
on the windowsill's bricked edge,
where did it come from?
Moving with the same ripple . . . As if,
audible in the ragged yearning,

visible in this tentative assertion of sun
on the lip of a window in Chelsea,
is a flake of that long waving
long ago lodged in you. All this light
traveled aeons to become 23rd Street,

and a hotel room in the late afternoon
—singular neon outside already
warm and quavering—and you in it,
sure now, because of the song
delivered to you, dealt to you

like an outcome, that there is
something stubborn in us
—does it matter how small it is?—
that does not diminish.
What is it? An ear,

a wave? Not a bud
or a cinder, not a seed
or a spark: something else:
obdurate, specific, insoluble.
Something in us does not erode.

PRINCIPALITIES OF JUNE

Original light broke apart,
the Gnostics say,
when time began,

singular radiance
fractioned into form
—an easy theory

to believe,
in early summer,
when that first performance

seems repeated daily.
Though wouldn't it mean
each fracturing took us

that much further
from heaven?
Not in this town,

not in June: harbor
and cloudbank, white houses'
endlessly broken planes,

a long argument
of lilac shadows and whites
as blue as noon:

phrasebooks of day,
articulated most of all
in these roses,

which mount and swell
in dynasties of bloom,
their easy idiom

a soundless compaction
of lip on lip. Their work,
these thick flowerheads?

Built to contain
sunlight, they interrupt
that movement just enough

to transfix in air, at eye level,
now: held still, and shattering,
which is the way with light:

the more you break it,
the nearer it comes to whole.

LILY AND BRONZE

Zenith June and this tower:
seventeen white throats
opening a tier at a time

to interiors purely narcotic—

I mean the lily's giddy spire,
each trumpet nothing
but intent to drench

in scent and pollen
any approaching face.
Look at them

the full flare of them,
and your looking empties out;

turn back and there they are
blazing: they go on arriving,
as if nothing ended but our attention.

Like those horses in Venice,
the Quadriga, four Roman horses
stolen to Constantinople,

robbed again to Venice,
mounted on the façade of the basilica
a thousand years

then brought in from
the chemical rain,
restless and looming

in a brick vault I entered
through a little door—
I, I say, but I wasn't then,

but suddenly bright faces tilted
just to one side, turbulent, breathing
and o for the speech to make you

the muscle and push of it,
a bronze mouth for the heft
and thunderhead,

sweat and fire of them—

It's the same with the lilies:
look hard enough and they hurry
ceaseless toward a place where

you are no longer standing,
their flanks also dusted
in scoured gold. Second only,

until the moment collapses
and you turn away. Though
they go on unfolding,

in a great arrested suspension: leap and stasis fused.

FISH R US

Clear sac
of coppery eyebrows
suspended in amnion,
not one moving—

A Mars
composed entirely
of single lips,
each of them gleaming—

this bag of fish
(have they really
traveled here like *this*?)
bulges while they

acclimate, presumably,
to the new terms
of the big tank
at Fish R Us. Soon

they'll swim out
into separate waters,
but for now they're
shoulder to shoulder

in this clear and
burnished orb, each fry
about the size of this line,
too many lines for any

bronzy antique epic,
a million of them,
a billion incipient citizens
of a goldfish Beijing,

a São Paolo,
a Mexico City.
They seem to have sense
not to move but hang

fire, suspended, held
at just a bit of distance
(a bit is all there is), all
facing outward, eyes

(they can't even blink)
turned toward the skin
of the sac they're in,
this swollen polyethylene.

And though nothing's
rippling but their gills,
it's still like looking up
into falling snow,

if all the flakes
were a dull, breathing gold,
as if they were streaming toward
—not us, exactly,

but what they'll be . . .
Perhaps they're small enough
—live sparks, for sale
at a nickel apiece—

that one can actually
see them transpiring:
they want to swim
forward, want to

eat, want to take place.
Who's going to know
or number or even see them all?

They pulse in their golden ball.

ESSAY: THE LOVE OF OLD HOUSES

A glow from rough-planed floorboards
knotted and grained and chestnut-hued,
and flecked in the pores with bits
of antique paint: whale oil and lead

for red; was it arsenic that made this green?
Remnants grace the pitted spots
where the sander wouldn't reach—
well, it could have, but what we wanted,

when we took the burr wheel's
unwieldy drum to these planks,
was to honor the whorls and curves
that made them themselves, variant,

well-used. Like skin. Fired just now
by afternoon pouring heat and honey
onto these wide swathes seasoned,
two centuries, to something durable,

too much an inhabitation of warmth
to qualify as inanimate—as though sunlight
softened their cooled, human store
and sent it wafting up like scent

from warmed wax. I know.
I am that firing light, and I'm the hand
that's oiled these boards
with a resin-and-varnish brew,

tincture that let these cello depths
emerge, and last. And so
what I've—we've—made is not
outside myself, not exactly;

rather it's a container—
sagging and shored, corroding
and replenished—in which one
doesn't need to hold oneself together:

relax, and oh, the rooms will do it for you.
It's safe to loosen our borders
here, and know ourselves housed.
I sanded and Danish-oiled

these floors with a man who's dead,
and the planks gleam still—
a visible form of vitality—
for you and I, love, who now revise,

as each inhabitant must,
the dwelling place. Making new
builds upon every layer come before;
we're joined to whoever

wore the stairstep down, or cracked
the corner of a windowpane, or waxed
these boards when company was coming.
Which is why I like old houses best:

here it's proved that time requires
a deeper, better verb than *pass*;
it's more like pool, and ebb, and double
back again, my history, his, yours,

subsumed into the steadying frame
of a phrase I love: *a building*:
both noun and verb, where we live
and what we do: fill it with ourselves,

all the way to the walls,
proximity made bearable by separate,
commingling privacies
that spill and meet at the edge

as clouds do, and together
comprise an atmosphere,
our place. What else is new?
A broom for you, a stack of rags

for me, our own old T-shirts cut
to squares and once again of use.
A tin of wax, these lovely smells:
tropic resins, petroleum.

AMERICAN SUBLIME

St. Johnsbury, Vermont

Closing time at the Athenaeum,
but this visitor bat
(who knows how he got in)
seems intent on staying the night;
our waving arms, a rolled Times,
the janitor's broom haven't fazed him a bit.

In flits and starts he swoops
in crazy eights from cornice to
pilaster, chandelier to book-
shelf top, finial to plaster-
work to pediment. He seems
especially to like the vast

painting he skims like a pond,
a Bierstadt prospect of Yosemite,
billboard for immensity. The painter's
out to correct our sense of scale:
grandeur meant not to diminish
but enlarge, as the eye hurries

up that cleft dome of rock
to hazy light, light made material,
crown of glory, a suffused
atmosphere intended to mean
intensely. Our adventurer
doesn't stop to look, careening

above this antique ad for fresh air
as though he owned it,
and these books and music stands
and brass easels which display
last century's genre paintings
leaning back, labeled, heavily framed.

What's more out of date, nature
or the representation of it?
A velvet dust-rag wing
brushes canvas, granite dome,
the varnished vastness,
then rests a beat on that bust of

—Emerson? And now we
visitors, though we've all enjoyed
the unexpected fluttery show,
give up. Time to go home.
Where did we park? Dim the lamps.
Last glance: bat and Bierstadt

all in the dark. Nothing. No,
there he is! Flying, just visible
in the faint signal of the exit sign:
our little hero circumambulating still
the gloss of oil, the polished pools
and waterfall, our rocks and rills.

SOURCE

I'd been traveling all day, driving north
—smaller and smaller roads, clapboard houses
startled awake by the new green around them—

when I saw three horses in a fenced field
by the narrow highway's edge: white horses,

two uniformly snowy, the other speckled
as though he'd been rolling in flakes of rust.
They were of graduated sizes

—small, medium, large—and two stood
to watch while the smallest waded

in a shallow pond,
tossing his head and taking
—it seemed unmistakable—delight

in the cool water around his hooves
and ankles. I kept on driving, I went into town

to visit the bookstores and the coffee bar,
and looked at the new novels
and the volumes of poetry, but all the time

it was horses I was thinking of,
and when I drove back to find them

the three companions left off
whatever it was they were playing at,
and came nearer the wire fence—

I'd pulled over onto the grassy shoulder
of the highway—to see what I'd brought them.

Experience is an intact fruit,
core and flesh and rind of it; once cut open,
entered, it can't be the same, can it?

Though that is the dream of the poem:
as if we could look out
through that moment's blushed skin.
They wandered toward the fence.
The tallest turned toward me;

I was moved by the verticality of her face,
elongated reach from the ear tips

down to white eyelids and lashes,
the pink articulation
of nostrils, wind stirring the strands

of her mane a little to frame the gaze
in which she fixed me. She was the bold one;

the others stood at a slight distance
while she held me in her attention.
Put your tongue to the green-flecked

peel of it, reader, and taste it
from the inside: Would you believe me
if I said that beneath them a clear channel

ran from the three horses to the place
they'd come from, the cool womb

of nothing, cave at the heart
of the world, deep and resilient and firmly set
at the core of things? Not emptiness,

not negation, but a generous, cold nothing:
the breathing space out of which new shoots

are propelled to the grazing mouths,
out of which horses themselves are tendered
into the new light. The poem wants the impossible;

the poem wants a name for the kind nothing
at the core of time, out of which the foals

come tumbling: curled, fetal, dreaming,
and into which the old crumple, fetlock
and skull breaking like waves of foaming milk . . .

Cold, bracing nothing, which mothers forth
mud and mint, hoof and clover, root hair

and horsehair and the accordion bones
of the rust-spotted little one unfolding itself
into the afternoon. You too: you flare

and fall back into the necessary
open space. What could be better than that?

It was the beginning of May,
the black earth nearly steaming,
and a scatter of petals decked the mud

like pearls, everything warm with setting out,
and you could see beneath their hooves
the path they'd traveled up, the horse-road

on which they trot into the world, eager for pleasure
and sunlight, and down which they descend,

in good time, into the source of spring.

from
SCHOOL OF THE
ARTS
(2005)

FLIT

        —dart—an idea
arcs the cold, then a clutch

of related thoughts;
slim branches don't even

flicker with the weight
of what's landed;

animate alphabet
whizzing past our faces,

a black and white hurry,
as if a form of notation

accompanied our walk,
a little ahead of us

and a bit behind. If we
could *see* their trajectory,

if their trace remained
in the winter air,

what a tunnel they'd figure:
skein of quick vectors

above our heads,
a fierce braid,

improvised, their decisions
—the way one makes poetry

from syntax—unpredictable, resolving
to wild regularity

(thought has to flit
to describe it, speech

has to try that hurry).
A scaffolding,

a kind of argument
about being numerous.

Thread and rethread—alight.
Study. We might be carrying

crumbs. We're not. I wish.
Their small heads cock,

they lift (no visible effort,
as if flight were the work

of the will only), light,
a bit further along,

and though they're silent
it seems you could hear

the minute repeating registers
of their attention,

*_____, *_____, the *here you are*
yes here you yes.

Pronoun reference unclear.
Who looks at us

—an aerial association
of a dozen subjectivities,

or a singular self
wearing, this snowy afternoon,

twelve pair of wings?
Collectivity of sparks,

sparking collectivity? Say *live*
resides not inside feathers or skin

but in the whizzing medium.
No third person.

Sharp, clear globe of January,
and we—the fourteen of us—

the thinking taking place.
We is instances of alertness,

grammar help me.
Mind in the ringing day,

a little of us ahead
and a bit behind,

and all that action
barely disturbs the air.

HEAVEN FOR STANLEY

For his birthday, I gave Stanley a hyacinth bean,
an annual, so he wouldn't have to wait for the flowers.

He said, *Mark, I have just the place for it!*
as if he'd spent ninety-eight years

anticipating the arrival of this particular vine.

I thought poetry a brace against time,
the hours held up for study in a voice's cool saline,

but his allegiance is not to permanent forms.
His garden's all furious change,

budding and rot and then the coming up again;

why prefer any single part of the round?
I don't know that he'd change a word of it;

I think he could be forever pleased
to participate in motion. Something opens.

He writes it down. Heaven steadies
and concentrates near the lavender. He's already there.

THE STAIRS

Back when Arden could still climb our stairs
—sharply pitched, turning near the top,
the sort old carpenters modeled on the stairways of ships—

he'd follow Paul up to his study, shadow me
up for socks or a clean shirt. Even if I only went upstairs

for a minute, he'd wheeze and labor on the narrow steps,
and arrive out of breath, proud of himself,
and collapse on the rug before coming down again.

Up and down, all day. At night, he wanted to sleep
in his bed at the foot of ours, wanted it so badly
the pressure intensified the climb,

what with the tall risers and his gimpy hind legs. So he cried,
and fussed, and tried, gave up and went away, came back

and tried again. If he couldn't make it on his own,
I'd get up and help him, lifting his front paws
and setting them into place, then my hands under his hips;

the stairwell would smell of his anxiety: bodily,
familiar, slightly acid. Once he could no longer climb

something so awkward, it was as if he'd forgotten
he ever wanted to; he'd wedge his muzzle
into a hole he'd made in the sliding screen door,

push it to the left, and sleep all night in the garden,
on the gravel beneath the spread of a Montauk daisy.

Why can't I hold on to that image: the dreamer
beneath black leaves and a spatter of summer stars?
Indelible, that old man scent,

the fear that makes the stairway steeper.

ULTRASOUND

Blackboard covered with a dust
   of living chalk, live chaos-cloud
      wormed by turbulence: the rod glides

and the vet narrates shadows
   I can't quite force into shape:
      His kidneys might . . . the spleen appears . . .

I can't see what he sees, and so
   resort to simile: cloudbank, galaxy
      blurred with slow comings

and goings, that far away. The doctor
   makes appreciative noises,
      to encourage me;

he praises Beau's stillness.
   I stroke the slope beneath
      those open, abstracted eyes,

patient, willing to endure whatever
   we deem necessary, while the vet
      runs along the shaved blond

—blue-veined, gleaming with gelled alcohol
   to allow sound to penetrate
      more precisely—a kind of wand,

pointing a stream of waves
   —nothing we could hear—
      to translate the dark inside his ribs

onto this midnight screen.
  The magic pen slides, the unseen's made—
    well, far from plain.

No chartable harmony,
  less anatomy than a storm
    of pinpoints subtler than stars.

Where does a bark upspool
  from the quick,
    a baritone swell

past the sounding chambers?
  You can't see that, or the clock
    built into the wellspring,

or that fixed place from which
  a long regarding of us
    rises. It wasn't cancer,

wasn't clear, we didn't see, really,
  anything. He's having trouble
    keeping up his weight;

his old appetites flag,
  though on the damp morning trails
    he's the same golden hurry.

Today I'm herding the two old dogs
  into the back of the car,
    after the early walk, wet woods:

Beau's generous attention must be
  brought into focus, gaze pointed
    to the tailgate so he'll be ready to leap,

and Arden, arthritic in his hind legs,
    needs me to lift first his forepaws
        and then, placing my hands

under his haunches, hoist the moist
    black bulk of him into the wagon,
        and he growls a little

before he turns to face me gratefully,
    glad to have been lifted—
        And as I go to praise them,

as I like to do, the words
    that come from my mouth,
        from nowhere, are *Time's children,*

as though that were the dearest thing
    a person could say.
        Why did I call them by that name?

They race this quick parabola
    faster than we do, as though
        it were a run in the best of woods,

run in their dreams, paws twitching
    —even asleep they're hurrying.
        Doesn't the world go fast enough for them?

We're caught in this morning's
    last-of-April rain, the three of us
        bound and fired by duration

—rhythm too swift for even them
    to hear, though perhaps we catch
        a little of that rush and ardor

—furious poetry!—
   the sound time makes,
      seeing us through.

IN THE SAME SPACE

The sun set early in the Square, winter afternoons,
angling over the apartments to the west, so that light would
    bisect

the northern row of dark houses diagonally, the grand houses
that were suddenly not of the last century but of the century
    before.

Then the world would seem equally divided, a while, between
    the golden
and the chill, equipoise in a bitter year. When the sun was
    completely gone,

we'd turn for home, the dogs and I, and to the south, the two
    towers,
harshly formal by day, brusque in their authority—

at the beginning of evening they'd go a blue a little darker than
    the sky,
lit from top to bottom by a wavering curtain of small, welcoming
    lamps.

HEAVEN FOR PAUL

The flight attendant said,
We have a mechanical problem with the plane,
and we have contacted the FAA for advice,

and then, *We will be making an emergency landing in Detroit,*

and then, *We will be landing at an air force base in Dayton,*
because there is a long runway there, and because
there will be a lot of help on the ground.

Her voice broke slightly on the word *help,*
and she switched off the microphone, hung it back on its hook,
turned to face those of us seated near her,
and began to weep.

Could the message have been more clear?
Around us people began to cry themselves,
or to pray quietly, or to speak to those with whom
they were traveling, saying the things that people
would choose to say to one another before
an impending accident of uncertain proportion.

It was impossible to hear, really, the details
of their conversations—it would have been wrong to try—
but we understood the import of the tones of voice
everywhere around us, and we turned to each other,

as if there should have been some profound things to be im-
    parted,
but what was to be said seemed so obvious and clear:
that we'd had a fine few years, that we were terrified
for the fate of our own bodies and each other's,
and didn't want to suffer, and could not imagine

the half hour ahead of us. We were crying a little
and holding each other's hands, on the armrest;
I was vaguely aware of a woman behind us, on the aisle,
who was startled at the sight of two men holding hands,

and I wondered how it could matter to her, now,
on the verge of this life—and then I wondered how it could
     matter to me,
that she was startled, when I flared on that same margin.

The flight attendant instructed us in how to brace
for a crash landing—to remove our glasses and shoes
and put our heads down, as we did long ago, in school,
in the old days of civil defense. We sat together, quietly.
And this is what amazed me: Paul,

who of the two of us is the more nervous,
the less steadily grounded in his own body,
became completely calm. Later he told me

how he visualized his own spirit
stepping from the flames, and visited,
in his mind's picturing, each person he loved,
and made his contact and peace with each one,

and then imagined himself turning toward
what came next, an unseeable *ahead*.
                                   For me,
it wasn't like that at all. I had no internal composure,

and any ideas I'd ever entertained about dying
seemed merely that, speculations flown now
while my mind spiraled in a hopeless sorrowful motion,

sure I'd merely be that undulant fuel haze
in the air over the runway, hot chemical exhaust,
atomized, no idea what had happened to me,

what to do next, and how much of the next life
would I spend (as I have how much of this one?)
hanging around an airport. I thought of my dog,

and who'd care for him. No heaven for me,
only the unimaginable shape of not-myself—
and in the chaos of that expectation,

without compassion, unwilling,
I couldn't think beyond my own dissolution.
What was the world without me to see it?
And while Paul grew increasingly radiant,

the flight attendant told us it was time to crouch
into the positions we had rehearsed,
the plane began to descend, wobbling,

and the tires screeched against the runway,
burning down all but a few feet of five miles of asphalt
before it rolled its way to a halt.

We looked around. We let go
the long-held breath, the sighs and exhalations,
Paul exhausted from the effort of transcendence,

myself too pleased to be breathing to be vexed
with my own failure, and we were still sitting and beginning to
    laugh
when the doors of the plane burst open,

and large uniformed firemen came rushing down the aisles,
shouting *Everybody off the plane, now, bring nothing with you,
leave the plane immediately,*

—because, as we'd learn in the basement
of the hangar where they'd brought us,
a line of tornadoes was scouring western Ohio,
approaching the runway we'd fled.

At this point it seemed plain: if God intervenes
in history, it's either to torment us
or to make us laugh, or both, which is how

we faced the imminence of our deaths the second time.
I didn't think once about my soul, as we waited in line,
filing into the hangar, down into the shelter

—where, after a long while, the National Guard would bring us
boxes and boxes of pizza, and much later, transport us, in buses,
to complimentary hotel rooms in Cincinnati.

SIGNAL

LOST COCKATIEL cried the sign, hand lettered,
taped to the side of a building: *last seen on 16th*

between Fifth and Sixth, gray body, orange cheek patches,
yellow head. Name: Omar. Somebody's dear, I guess,

though how do you lose a cockatiel on 16th Street?
Flown from a ledge, into the sky he's eyed

for months or years, into the high limbs of the gingkos,
suddenly free? I'm looking everywhere in the rustling

globes and spires shot through with yellow,
streaking at the edges, for any tropic flash of him. Why

should I think I'd see him, in the vast flap this city is?
Why wander Chelsea when that boy could be up and gone,

winging his way to Babylon or Oyster Bay,
drawn to some magnet of green. Sense to go south?

Not likely; Omar's known the apartment and the cage,
picked his seeds from a cup, his fruits and nuts from the hand

that anchored him—and now, he's launched, unfindable,
no one's baby anymore but one bit . . .

Think of the great banks of wires and switches
in the telephone exchange, every voice and signal

a little flicker lighting up—that's Omar now,
impulse in the propulsive flow. Who'll ever know?

Then this morning we're all in the private commuter blur
when a guy walks onto the subway car

doing bird calls, decked in orange and lime,
a flag pluming his baseball cap; he's holding out a paper cup

while he shifts from trills to caws. Not much of a talent,
I think, though I like his shameless attempt at charm,

and everybody's smiling covertly, not particularly tempted
to give him money. Though one man reaches into his pocket

and starts to drop some change into the cup,
and our Papageno says, "That's my coffee, man,

but thanks, God bless you anyway,"
and lurches whistling out the door.

FIRE TO FIRE

All smolder and oxblood,
these flowerheads,
flames of August:

fierce bronze,
or murky rose,
petals concluded in gold—

And as if fire called its double down

the paired goldfinches
come swerving quick
on the branching towers,

so the blooms
sway with the heft
of hungers

indistinguishable, now,
from the blossoms.

◆　◆　◆

Tannic yellow, or rust,

a single brassy streak
at each mid-petal
colluding in a bull's-eye ring,

copper circle
around the seed-horde
flashing like a solar flare.

You can't finish looking:
they rear and wave
in pentecostal variety.

You might as well be tracing flames.

✦　✦　✦

Maybe nothing gold
can stay separate—
not feather flower fire.
My work's to say
what signals here,
but Lord I cannot
see a single thing.

✦　✦　✦

If I were a sunflower I would be
the branching kind,

my many faces held out
in all directions, all attention,

awake to any golden
incident descending;

drinking in the world

with my myriads of heads,
I'd be my looking.

✦　✦　✦

Painters have painted their swarming groups and the centre-figure
     of all,
From the head of the centre-figure spreading a nimbus of gold-color'd
     light,
But I paint myriads of heads, but paint no head without its nimbus of
     gold color'd light . . .

    ♦   ♦   ♦

Their rattling August clothes,
faces a swirl of hours,
                              coil in the seed
unwound at last to these
shag faces bent
over the ruining garden:

Warm evening,
                    vertical
and gold,

stalk of the body,
glistening hairs
radiating out from the curled

& lifted leaves

paired along the stalk, pattern
plunging toward the center
like the line of the thighs . . .

    ♦   ♦   ♦

Paul said when the neighbor's puppy
ran across the street, into traffic,
because it wanted to see our dogs,
it looked like "a little flame."

♦ ♦ ♦

Nothing gold can stand
apart from any other; the sunflowers are trafficked

by birds, open to bees and twilight,
implicated, alert: fire longs to meet itself
flaring, longing wants
a multiplicity of faces,

branching and branching out,

heads mouths eyes
wishing always to
double their own heat.

Which is why the void can make nothing lasting:

the fuse resides in the yellow candling up, signaling,
and the concomitant yellow hurrying down to meet it,

and nothing that is fixed
can call its double down from heaven;
                                        the gold calls to the gold
in the arc and rub,
calls to itself in the other,
                            which is why
the corona'd seedhead flashes the finches down.

from THE VAULT

1. The Bootblack

What can be said of this happiness?
The bootblack boy on his knees
in the dim of the bar gives himself
completely to the work of polishing,

leaning into the body on the stool
before him, a shirtless and eager man
who's being mouthed clean.
Around them parts the human dark.

Not much to do with degradation;
the generous bootblack pours
his attention out of his body
—all alertness—into the presence

before him, up the legs, beautiful,
burying his face in the warm cloth
of the lap: completed, receptacle,
recipient, held, filled—

Though it's hardly passive:
he's working to relinquish,
giving the seated one pleasure,
releasing his own weight.

They seem to light the gloom
of their corner; together
they make one lamp. And as if
his work were not complete

until it had been seen by another
—labor of the mouth,
art perfected with the tongue—
he turns his face up toward me,

his witness, smiling, though the verb's
thin for this unshielded triumph
of a face: What's he conquered?
Distance and dissatisfaction have slipped

from the look he lifts to me,
so that his power might not go
unacknowledged, now that
he is the image of achieved joy.

2. Double Embrace

Skin to the back of me,
skin to the fore,

and I'm at the center
of a double embrace,

or perhaps that's not
the precise term,

since no one's
face to face; we are

three shirtless men
become one

tentative whole,
the thick arms behind me

pressing against my arms,
then reaching forward

to the arms before me,
drawing us tighter together,

heat and slow
uprush of it; no hurry,

the embrace rocking
a bit, a bit of motion

to bind three disparate
bodies into—Look what we can make!

Six arms snaking,
so that the darkened barroom

recedes, and the mirrors,
the pendant lanterns and bluish

video haze. Then the firm hands
kneading my shoulders, hands

over my heart, my hands
on the shoulders in front of me,

those arms reached back toward
the original arms, as though

we were the chain of generation,
each man proceeding from the one

before, and each also reaching
backward, into the body

which had borne him—
The bar's a cave of minor

miracle played out—
it's not sex I want, if what sex is

is coming; more than that,
search and pleasure, reading,

divining signals, shift of attention,
flare in my direction, pose,

tattooed arms gleaming, hips
cocked in their particular invitation.

Particular! We're almost generalized
here, local avatars

of a broader principle,
we are just now representative men

doing the men's work
—fierce vulnerability—

open and containing, open
and held, the forward momentum

ceased, swaying a little, a few minutes
before the triangle breaks apart.

belly hard in the small of my back,
kiss to the back of my neck,

and I lean forward to kiss
the neck before me.

7. The Blessing

They were deep in the mine of souls
—no, I mean they'd gone far
into that shaft where inner and outer

grow indissoluble, dark against dark,
say beneath a bridge at night, where long attention
allows a sense of the breathing rippling;

they were practicing, heavy boots
above them, moving a little, above the grid
of a floor like those of stacked prison cells

—a brig, a Piranesian chamber, a cavern of men—

they were immersed in the night
when something warm—at first they knew not
what, they had no understanding, in the darkness—

another—sudden droplet—*small rain*—
Reader, I have no adequate term
for what blessed them, no word commensurate . . .

Then he conceived what he could:
a notion: if he remained in his body

(contained within
the bond of a perimeter
simultaneously fixed and permable,

if he were stayed, if he held fast—)

then he would break into flower.

THE PINK POPPY

                          opened in the night,
just one blossom, and when you step out
into the new air it "takes your breath away,"
as beauty is said to do: suddenly

you're flaring, open
at the top of yourself as the petals are, loose,
fringed at the edges, their interior

splotched a black already fading
toward plum, fringe and flare
wavering, in the rain,

early storm
—four-part thunder . . .
That pink lip held up

while heaven turns
in on itself, rumbling—

   ◆ ◆ ◆

But there—you aren't supposed
to talk about beauty, are you?

   ◆ ◆ ◆

Poor Arden's hiding under my desk;
when the thunder comes he seems to constrict himself,
and then a few moments later he's breathing heavily,

deaf as he is, holding himself taut in vigilance.
The poppy's erect
and undulant in the rain;

a sort of terrestrial jellyfish,
wavering blot like a shape on an old film,
light spot in the eye after something bright,

ragged central polyp of seed
—dark nipple-colored anemone—
held up like a sexual display:

Blake: *Exuberance is Beauty*.

✦ ✦ ✦

Grace catches you out like a hook,
you're pulled out of yourself, a moment,

and that's the ache: peculiar blow,
reminded you aren't who you think you are.

To join oneself to this breathing pink chalice—

You want more than that?

✦ ✦ ✦

A fire with a darkness in the center,
rippling interstices of night and flame . . .

Incorporated in a radiant vitality:

you want more than that?

*   *   *

Dangerous, to hate the thing that brings you all of this:
that flower wouldn't blaze if time didn't burn,

my golden dog rusting now under the roof of the garden
wouldn't have been either—no flecked ruffle
of the jowl, inner lip pink and loose . . .

And Arden: old pink muzzle sniffing now at the rain.

Brief, but no one wishes it never

*   *   *

Theories of Beauty

1. Hook that pulls us out of time

2. or a lure to catch us in it

3. Rupture in the boundary
    caused by delight, recognition of what
    we aren't, then suddenly are?

4. Longing solidified

5. Flaunts some flaw
    —evanescence, radical pink—
    and owns that quality
    so firmly it triumphs

6. Rilke: *You, you only, exist.*
   We pass away, till at last,
   our passing is so immense
   that you arise: beautiful moment,
   in all your suddenness . . .

7. The moment budded out of us?

♦ ♦ ♦

Pink fist.   Iron frill.

Essential frippery.   Fierce embroidery.

Core decor.   Severe extravagance.

Lip of otherness.   Evidence.

♦ ♦ ♦

It was the pink crown of hellfire,
(if hell means traffic in time)

arisen out of the earth in spring;

the vernal breaking-out
of the underglow,

and you wanted to touch it,
to be instructed by those flames
—cool and tempting—

and in a while, the rain bent
the stem to the gravel.

HEAVEN FOR ARDEN

Back when Arden could still go for a walk—a real walk,

not the twenty yards or so
he stumbles and lurches now—

he used to be anxious and uncertain, looking to me,

stopping awhile, tentatively, to see if I'd agree
to go no further, sometimes whining a bit

in case I'd respond. Sooner or later,

the turn would come; we'd gone far enough
for one day. Joy! As if he'd been afraid all along

this would be the one walk that would turn out to be infinite.

Then he could take comfort
in the certainty of an ending,

and treat the rest of the way as a series of possibilities;
then he could run,

and find pleasure in the woods beside the path.

NOTEBOOK/ TO LUCIEN FREUD/ ON THE VEIL

I love starting things

◆ ◆ ◆

Fat and shadow, oil and wax,
mobility solidified,
like cooled grease in a can—

◆ ◆ ◆

Seeing how far I can go

◆ ◆ ◆

      Analiese said, happily, "He paints the ugliness of flesh,"
      but that isn't it: flesh without the overlayer, how we
ought to see it, all we're taught—
      January sky over Seventh. To the north,
      a slab of paraffin. A wax table. Then it pinks,

      shifts, at the most complicated hour, after sunset, before
dark, the lamps already on.
      A deepening blue at the sky's center, but the tops of the
buildings still warmed by the last of sunlight,
      the way he fixes the face at its most subtle hour

◆ ◆ ◆

One of the things that makes you continue is the difficulty surely

◆ ◆ ◆

all the decisions of color revealed, light making available
every nuance of a (sur)face so plainly itself it's become plea and
testament.

Ugly: refuse the term, or open it: the living edge resisting?
Surface the heart of the matter.
Strange achievement: to see skin
as no one else.

◆　◆　◆

Never any beauty

greater than the body hung in the ceaseless wind of time
and repeating in that current its stream of postures,

skin perpetually lit from within
as if by its own failure—

◆　◆　◆

When I paint clothes I am really painting naked people who are
　　covered in clothes

◆　◆　◆

January in grisaille.
　　　Sarah and Lucy erased,
　　　　　　weirdly euphonious terms:

lymphoma, heroin.
　　　Then an anonymous body
　　　　　　on the sidewalk,

a fifth-floor room onto Sixth Avenue,
          the aching window open all afternoon.
                    A man on our block

pulled from his car and beaten
          with a tire-iron by another driver
                    who wanted him to hurry up

and pass the garbage truck.
          Flesh fails and failure
                    is visited upon it.

The book of Freud's paintings
          a brooding invitation, catalogue
                    of human suspension in time

and today I think they're an oil
          and pigment howl,
                    outpouring against limit.

But as soon as I've said it,
          the old argument resumes,
                    the ambiguity of *vanitas*:

do these paintings of dying things
          warn or celebrate,

does their maker caution or consume?

My life in the fields of this argument,

shifting skin
                    the live veil,

                    elongated grammar of muscle,

this moment's agreement of light

on the pure actual. (No such thing as *the* body.)

Fact of a wrist.

Vein troubling a forehead.

Melville: *How can the prisoner reach outside except by thrusting*
   through the wall?

◆ ◆ ◆

                              (By the waterfountain in
                              the gym)

On the huge man's left arm TRUST
above an image he called the god of joy
on his right forearm
inscribed above the veins
a centaur

symbol of leadership he said
of direction

I couldn't speak, in some deep basement of myself thinking
Maybe his great body is the fact

I require . . .

the dream of being *realized*

And half the night I'm thinking
of the immense human wall
and veil of him. What is it
we want from a body;

the lying-awake longing,
to what does it attend? Whitman:
These thoughts in the darkness why are they?

◆ ◆ ◆

Clothing veils
the real;
        flesh conceals—

what to call it?
quick lively presence quickening
through the lidded eyes,

a moment's sharp attention,

the painting looking back at us?

◆ ◆ ◆

The mystery isn't mind
        (what else are we, evidently,
        besides *aware?*)

but materiality, intersection
        of solidity and flame,
        where quick and stillness meet—

Materiality the impenetrable thing.
                    We don't know what it *is*
                    other than untrustworthy—

all bodies, even the young,
                    who rightly think
                    they're untouchable:

that faith's their signature
                    and credential.
                    I am a body less reliable,

and therefore the rough-scumbled peaks
                    of these faces thrill, familiar—
                    aspects of flesh breaking here,

the way we say waves break—
                    become visible at the instant
                    of their descent.

Caught somewhere in the arc.
                    How will these look
                    in a hundred years?

Stunningly here.

           ◆   ◆   ◆

Intricate wall
of appearances—

                    lit at its highest entablatures,

water towers and rooftops, cornice and capital,
                    smokestack and chimneypot picked out

by the glow slanting across the river,
                              intensified Hudson-light,

and warm lamps in the high windows,
                              neon over the shopfronts

flickering on;

world of consummate detail.

The city lay back,
shambling, corpulent, nude . . .
                              (why he loves the big frame:

because it is no longer
                    flesh
                    but *the* flesh)

   ◆ ◆ ◆

Nothing ever stands in for anything. Nobody is representing
   anything.

   ◆ ◆ ◆

My god: every body
of a piece, every factual expanse of skin,
the contour of them—

that's what language can't do, curve and heft of it,
that stretch . . . Oil and shadow,
fat and wax, grief solidified.

There's no one else.
You and I the common apprehension of this.

♦ ♦ ♦

Our chests open, arms back,
the teacher said, "This is a position
of fierce vulnerability—"

I thought, that's it, that's
exactly a position one could live
toward, to stand in permeable faith,

and yet such force in that stance,
upright, heart thrust out
to the world, unguarded, no hope

without the possibility of a wound.
"To hold oneself in this pose," he said,
"takes incredible strength."

♦ ♦ ♦

Everything is autobiographical

♦ ♦ ♦

I look at his pictures and want
above all language muscling up,
active work of pushing out some sound,
throat and muscle of the tongue,

some hope of accuracy—

♦ ♦ ♦

and everything is a portrait, even if it's a chair

◆ ◆ ◆

Accuracy? Go on, then—

to write the tragedy of this body

◆ ◆ ◆

I want to go on until there is nothing more to see

Notes

Rilke's "Orpheus. Eurydice. Hermes," in which Rilke writes that the lament of Orpheus for Eurydice is such that from it arises a world of lamentation, and above that a "lament-heaven, with its own disfigured stars."

ATLANTIS

Atlantis: *The section entitled "Michael's Dream" is for Michael Trombley, Stephen Housewright, Maggie Valentine, Carlos Melendez, and Marie Howe. The section entitled "Coastal" is for Darren Otto.*

Tunnel Music: *For Philip Levine.*

Homo Will Not Inherit: *For Michael Carter.*

Migratory: *After Hayden Carruth's "No Matter What, After All, and That Beautiful Word So."*

Nocturne in Black and Gold: *Titled after Whistler.*

Grosse Fuge: *For Robert Shore, 1948–1993.*

SWEET MACHINE

Door to the River: *Titled after Willem de Kooning's 1960 painting in the collection of the Whitney Musuem of American Art.*

White Kimono: *Lynda Hull, 1954–1994; and Wally Roberts, 1951–1994.*

Shelter: *For Michael Carter.*

Lilies in New York: *For Jorie Graham. Titled after a drawing by Jim Dine.*

Golden Retrievals: *For Robert Jones, spoken by Beau.*

Lilacs in NYC: *Owes the notion of the department store as an "available version of infinity" to an essay by Eric Zencey, "Xeno's Mall," from his book* Virgin Forest.

Mercy on Broadway: *Titled after a song by Laura Nyro.*

SCHOOL OF THE ARTS

Flit: *Black-capped chickadee*, Poecile atricapilla.

Heaven for Stanley: *For Stanley Kunitz, 1905–2006.*

The Stairs:

> . . . *But when he heard*
> *Odysseus' voice nearby, he did his best*
> *to wag his tail, nose down, with flattened ears,*
> *having no strength to move nearer his master . . .*
> (Homer, *The Odyssey*, translated by Robert Fitzgerald).

Ultrasound: *The job of the living is to be seen through* (Brenda Hillman).

In the Same Space: *Titled after Edmund Keeley and Philip Sherard's translation of C. P. Cavafy's poem, which reads, in its entirety:*

The setting of houses, cafes, the neighborhood
that I've seen and walked through years on end:

I created you while I was happy, while I was sad,
with so many incidents, so many details.

And, for me, the whole of you has been transformed
into feeling.

Heaven for Paul: *What do you mean, I am the more nervous?(Paul).*
Signal: *See www.markdoty.org/id13.html.*
Fire to Fire: *The italicized passage is from Whitman's "To You."*
The Vault:
And Craving said,
Why do you lie, since you belong to me?
(The Gospel According to Mary Magdalene,
translated by Jean-Yves Leloup and Joseph Rowe).
The first line of "The Blessing" is from Stephen Mitchell's translation of
Rilke's "Orpheus. Eurydice. Hermes." The final sentence recasts the con-
clusion of James Wright's poem "A Blessing."
Notebook/To Lucian Freud/ On the Veil: *Italicized passages not otherwise*
credited are quotations from the painter found in William Feaver's Lucian
Freud. *The Melville quotation is from* Moby-Dick, *the Whitman from*
"Song of the Open Road."

Acknowledgments

I owe thanks, for help with these nearly twenty-five years' worth of poems, to more people than I can possibly name. Suffice to say that this book wouldn't exist without the help of Richard Shelton, Charles Simic, David Wojahn, Lynda Hull, Kathryn Davis, Carol Muske Dukes, Lucie Brock-Broido, Marie Howe, James Hall, Thomas Lux, and Kathleen Graber. My thanks to many responsive readers for courage and heart. Gratitude to four wonderful editors, Robert Jones, Robin Robertson, Allison Callahan, and Terry Karten. And to David R. Godine, The University of Illinois Press, The National Poetry Series, Philip Levine, Bill Clegg, Ari Banias, and Julia Felsenthal. And most of all to two men who've made my life what it is, Wally Roberts and Paul Lisicky: *We go all the way up to the top of the night.*

Credits

The new poems in this volume have appeared in the following journals:

Alaska Quarterly: "Apparition (Oracular pear . . .)."

American Poetry Review: "Theory of the Sublime."

Bayou: "Angel of Prague."

Bloom: "Apparition (Handsome chest . . .)."

Ecotone: "Theory of Beauty (Grackles on Montrose)."

Five Points: "Apparition (Favorite Poem)"; "Magic Mouse"; "Theory of Beauty (Pompeii)"; "Theory of Narrative"; "Apparition (Chilly noon . . .)."

Harvard Divinity Bulletin: "Theory of Multiplicity."

The London Review of Books: "Theory of Beauty (Greenwich Avenue)."

Lumina: "Theory of Incompletion."

Magma: "Citizens."

McSweeney's: "Theory of Beauty (Tony)."

Ploughshares: "Pipistrelle."

Prairie Schooner: "Theory of Marriage."

Runes: "Theory of the Soul."

Triquarterly: "To Joan Mitchell"; "In the Airport Marshes."
Water-Stone Review: "The Word."

Grateful acknowledgment is made for permission to reprint the following poems:

From *Turtle, Swan*, copyright © 1987 by Mark Doty, reprinted by permission of David R. Godine, Publisher, Inc.: "Turtle, Swan"; "Charlie Howard's Descent."

From *Bethlehem in Broad Daylight*, copyright © 1991 by Mark Doty, reprinted by permission of David R. Godine, Publisher, Inc.: "Ararat"; "Six Thousand Terra-Cotta Men and Horses"; "Adonis Theatre."

From *My Alexandria*, copyright © 1995 by Mark Doty, used with permission of the University of Illinois Press: "The Advent Calendars"; "With Animals"; "*Esta Noche*"; "Human Figures"; "Days of 1981"; "Broadway"; "Demolition"; "Fog"; "Night Ferry"; "Lament-Heaven"; "The Ware Collection of Glass Flowers and Fruit, Harvard Museum"; "Difference"; "Almost Blue"; "Chanteuse"; "Bill's Story"; "Brilliance"; "No."

From *C. P. Cavafy: Collected Poems*, copyright © 1975, English translation by Edmund Keeley and Philip Sherrard, reprinted by permission of Princeton University Press: "In the Same Space."